DESIGNED FOR DESTINY

DESIGNED FOR DESTINY
Jerry H. Combee and Cline E. Hall

Tyndale House Publishers, Inc.   Wheaton, Illinois

The following publishers have given permission to use quotations from copyrighted works: From *An Interpretation of the English Bible: Revelation,* by B. H. Carroll., Copyright 1973. Used by permission of Baker Book House. From *A Christian America: Protestant Hopes and Historical Realities,* by Robert Handy. Copyright 1971. Used by permission of Oxford University Press. From *The Fundamentalist Phenomenon,* by Jerry Falwell with Ed Dobson and Ed Hindson. Copyright 1981. Used by permission of Doubleday & Co., Inc. From *The Last Days of America,* by Paul Erdman. Copyright 1981. Used by permission of Pocket Books.

Cover photo by Robert McKendrick

First printing, August 1985

Library of Congress Catalog Card Number 85-50490
ISBN 0-8423-0619-6
Copyright © 1985 Jerry H. Combee and Cline E. Hall
All rights reserved
Printed in the United States of America

CONTENTS

Introduction   7

PART ONE: A REVOLUTION IN RELIGION

1. Our Spiritual Founding Fathers   15
2. A Surprising Work of God   17
3. It Made America . . . America   20
4. Separation of Church and State   21
5. Liberty and Equality   24
6. One Nation under God   26
7. Destiny and Mission   27
8. The Real American Revolution   29

PART TWO: THE RELIGION OF REVOLUTION

9. The True Permanent Revolution   35
10. Rooted in Religious Convictions   38
11. The Laws of Nature and Nature's God   41
12. The American Civil Religion   45
13. The Doctrines of Democracy   47

Part Three: Mine Eyes Have Seen the Glory

14. "The Battle Hymn of the Republic" 51
15. An Irresistible Revolution 54
16. The Devil's Time Is Nearly Out 60
17. Doers of the Word 63
18. From Philanthropy to Politics 67
19. Let Us Die to Make Men Free 73

Part Four: Over There!

20. To Make the World Safe for Democracy 77
21. Manifest Destiny 80
22. The Vengeful Providence of God 84
23. The Ark of the Liberties of the World 87

Part Five: Decade of Destiny

24. From Mission to Malaise 93
25. A Moment of Silent Prayer 97
26. A Secular Society 99
27. The President as High Priest and Prophet 102
28. Secular Humanism 105
29. Reagan's Religious Rhetoric 107
30. The Evil Empire 109
31. East of Eden 113
32. A New Dawning for America 115

Notes 119
Appendix 123
Speech by President Ronald Reagan at the Forty-First Annual Convention of the National Association of Evangelicals, Sheraton Twin Towers Hotel, Orlando, Florida, March 8, 1983

INTRODUCTION

America of late has seemingly lost its momentum, a momentum that has been one of the keys to its national success.

As a group we have always been headed "somewhere." Our people have believed that something good lay ahead. A faith in progress and a confidence that the future of our children will be better than ours are the factors which have driven us on.

Gradually, we have been losing that faith. A crisis of confidence now seems to be striking at our national will and sapping our national energy. The confidence in the future that supported everything else—public institutions, private enterprise, our families, even the Constitution—that confidence has begun to fade as our vision of the future has dimmed.

"Where there is no vision, the people perish,"

declares the Bible. Our recent history has borne out the truth of this maxim.

To fill the void of vision in our country, religious leaders have rushed in, reminding us of our religious roots.

But a great debate has broken out over America's "Christian origins." Surprisingly, strong disagreement over this issue has emerged within the evangelical Christian community itself.

On the one side stand such writers as Peter Marshall and David Manuel in the widely read book *The Light and the Glory* (Fleming H. Revell, 1977). They contend that America was once a "Christian nation," and that it can be so again. They consider America to be a uniquely "chosen nation"—the "New Israel" of the modern era.

On the other side, well-known Christian scholars George Marsden, Nathan Hatch, and Mark Noll argue that America never has been and never can be a "Christian nation." In *The Search for Christian America* (Crossway Books, 1983), they question whether God has any plan or purpose for America, or has "chosen" it for a special task.

We disagree with both sides on the issue. We reject the way the question has been framed and the terms defined.

If you don't know what you're looking for, you won't know when you've found it.

America has never been, nor should it ever be, a "Christian nation" in the sense of a Christian version of the Ayatollah Khomeini's "Islamic republic" in Iran. The Bible should not be crammed down the throats of unbelievers the way Khomeini uses the Koran, the holy book of the religion of Islam.

Surprisingly, both what we would call the "right evangelicals" represented by *The Light and the Glory* and the "left evangelicals" represented by *The Search for Christian America* agree on what a truly "Christian nation" would be—a theocracy: the rule of Christians, by Christians, for Christians. They differ only over whether this is what America has ever been, and can or should be in the future.

We question the term "Christian nation," but if we used it, we would call a nation or civilization "Christian" only if it proclaims the principles of human equality and human rights and strives for religious and civil liberty for all its citizens.

Admittedly, no single Bible verse can be used as a proof text for these "doctrines of democracy." Nor does one have to be a "born-again" believer to see the truth of these moral ideals. Many of our Founding Fathers who were not Christians could, nevertheless, see the validity of these ideas that the Declaration of Independence calls "self-evident truths."

On the other hand, a society in which the Bible is preached is much more likely to reflect these truths in its national life. They are insights of which the world had only very imperfect knowledge before the first advent of Christ.

Hence the importance of the "Great Awakening" in American history, the spiritual revival that swept America before the revolution. That is where our book begins—with the "revolution in religion" that led to what we call the "religion of revolution," the spiritual and moral concepts stated in the Declaration of Independence. From that point, we move on to show how subsequent American history reflects the working out of the logic of these ideas.

America is not a "chosen nation" or a "New Israel," except perhaps in some very figurative sense. God has but one chosen people, the Jews, to whom His promises remain as valid as they ever were.

But God deals with nations just as surely as He deals with individuals. God did so in Old Testament times, and He continues to do so in New Testament times.

Yes, the Christian religion has such concerns about the individual and his salvation, and Christ is the only gate through which we may walk to get to the other side.

However, with nations the issue is not salvation but preservation. God in His sovereignty holds all nations—whether predominantly Christian, Jewish, or Muslim—to account against the moral law of the universe.

Some would disparage this notion of the relation of God and nations as "civil religion," and castigate it as "watered-down" Christianity. We recognize the danger of mistaking the religion of the nation for the plan of salvation. But the term "civil religion" strikes us as a perfectly good name for a very valid religious concept.

We hear much discussion today of the "Deism" of some of our Founding Fathers. "Deism" was the belief that in the beginning God created the world, but then sort of stepped out of the way and let it run by itself.

Many of our Christian brethren today strike us as "evangelical Deists," at least when it comes to history. They act as if during the period between

Christ's two advents, God has drawn away from the world to let history "sort of" run its course and the nations are not governed by His providence.

With George Bancroft (1800–1891), one of America's greatest historians, we contend that "the fortunes of a nation are not under the control of blind destiny," and that "a favoring providence, calling our institutions into being, has conducted the country to its present happiness and glory."[1]

A rebirth of the American spirit appears underway, at least in politics and economics. A host of great thinkers—George Gilder, Michael Novak, Milton Friedman—have written books for the general public extolling limited government and free enterprise.

But no one has dealt adequately with the concept of history that has been the impetus for the American spirit. That is the purpose of *Designed for Destiny*.

American history is part of a divine design.

The final act of the grand drama in which we are cast has yet to be played. We don't have the full script.

But we know our story has been writ by the very finger of God.

PART ONE

A REVOLUTION IN RELIGION

*What do we mean by the American Revolution...?
The Revolution was effected before the war commenced.
The Revolution was in the hearts and minds of the
people.*[1] John Adams

1 ★ OUR SPIRITUAL FOUNDING FATHERS

In the half century or so before the American Revolution, a spiritual revival swept America.

The Great Awakening, as the movement came to be known, did not result from the plots, plans, or programs of men. Those touched—numbering in many multiples of thousands—experienced what they believed to be a spontaneous outflow of the Spirit of God.

The preachers of the Great Awakening belong in our national gallery of heroes along with such men as Franklin, Washington, and Jefferson. In their own eyes, these preachers were mere instruments of a Higher Power, but in a deeper sense they were America's *spiritual founding fathers—the leaders of a true revolution in religion.*

Through the sermons of these pious men, Americans sensed the power of God working in the world: changing lives, controlling the course of nature, and above all, directing the flow of history.

A vivid vision of history captured the imagination of Americans.

Today, many consider history little more than, to quote Shakespeare, "a tale told by an idiot, full of sound and fury signifying nothing."

But to the generation of the Great Awakening, history appeared to be a reasonable, intelligent, and meaningful process, under the control of an infinite, rational Mind. Every event seemed to be a piece of a master plan, and America's destiny part of a divine design.

The distinctively American consciousness of history was born . . .

Optimism about the future . . .

Confidence in Providence . . .

The conviction that no enterprise, if conceived in accordance with the will of God, is too difficult to accomplish . . .

Vast new vistas opening up . . .

America today . . . tomorrow the world!

2 ★ A SURPRISING WORK OF GOD

In the 1730s America had sunk to a spiritual low.

The powerful piety of the Pilgrims and the Puritans had faded with the generations. Nominal Christianity prevailed—religion in name only.

Yet the tide of faith had no sooner ebbed when, to the surprise of many, a wave of national revival swept the land. "The Spirit of God began extraordinarily to set in,"[2] wrote Jonathan Edwards, the leading American preacher of the Great Awakening.

Englishman George Whitefield, who made seven evangelistic swings through the colonies, actually reached many more people than Edwards did. Whitefield became the best-known man in colonial America during the mid-1700s. He is said to have preached around eighteen thousand sermons to more than ten million people during his total ministry in America and the British Isles—and that in the age before microphones or mass media.

The key to Whitefield's outreach was open-air preaching. What television has meant to evangelism in the twentieth century, "field preaching" proved to be in the eighteenth.

But Jonathan Edwards was by far the intellectual giant, the great mind of the Great Awakening. His *Faithful Narrative of the Surprising Work of God* became the classic description of the nature and effect of religious revival:

There was scarcely a single person in the town, old or young, left unconcerned about the great things of the eternal world. Those who were wont to be the vainest, and loosest, and those who had been most disposed to think, and speak slightly of . . . religion, were now generally subject to great awakenings. And the work of conversion was carried on in a most astonishing manner, and increased more and more; souls did . . . come by flocks to Jesus Christ. From day to day, for many months together, might be seen evident instances of sinners brought out of darkness into marvelous light, and delivered out of a horrible pit . . . and set upon a rock with a new song of praise to God in their mouths.

This work of God, as it was carried on, and the number of true saints multiplied, soon made a glorious alteration in the town; so that in the spring and summer following, anno 1735, the town seemed to be full of distress, as it was then. There were remarkable tokens of God's presence in almost every house. It was a time of joy in families on account of salvation being brought unto them; parents rejoicing over their children as new born, and husbands over their wives, and wives over their husbands.[3]

Edwards was describing the results of the Great Awakening in the town of Northampton, Massachusetts. But it was discovered that *the same thing was happening simultaneously in other towns, without any human communication between them.*

During the 1740s, what had begun in Northampton spread to all of colonial America, from New England to Georgia, and even across the seas.

Edwards' *Faithful Narrative of the Surprising Work of God* was read in many places beyond America. It was read in England and on the European continent, where it gave people both a concrete idea of what a true spiritual awakening is and the hope that they, too, might experience one.

John Wesley, the great English evangelist, read it. England's "Great Evangelical Revival" broke out and turned the country upside down.

Revival broke out on the continent, too.

What had started in America was spreading to the world.

3 ★ IT MADE AMERICA ... AMERICA

The Great Awakening had incalculable spiritual effects on America and the world. During the revival, massive numbers of Americans were converted to Christianity. The Awakening also marked the effective beginning of modern mass evangelism and outreach that would soon grow into world missions—efforts, on an unprecedented scale, to take the Christian gospel to all mankind.

Was the Great Awakening a purely "religious" phenomenon? By no means. The revival reached deep into the American soul and decisively determined "the American mind."

Basic beliefs, vital to the American way of life, were burned into the consciousness of the American people. The Great Awakening actually made America into the unique nation that it was designed and destined to be.

The Great Awakening made America ... America!

4 ★ SEPARATION OF CHURCH AND STATE

By and large, the Great Awakening was opposed by the "mainline" churches of the day. And many of those churches were government controlled and financed, official, and "established," such as the Congregational Church in Massachusetts and the Episcopal (Anglican) Church in Virginia.

Many born-again Christians began to think that government had no business in the affairs of religion, that church and state ought to be kept separate and distinct.

When government tries to "establish" Christianity through legal and political means, it is really trying to do the impossible. It only creates confusion about the free heart belief, the inward persuasion of the mind, the "new birth" experience that is the essence of true and saving religion. During the Great Awakening, it was revealed that many of the pastors in the pulpits of the "established" churches were themselves unconverted!

22 A REVOLUTION IN RELIGION

The lesson of the Great Awakening was that Christians ought to favor church-state separation, not because it hinders, but because it helps the cause of genuine Christianity.

The Great Awakening thus helped to fix separation of church and state as a basic American belief and a cardinal tenet of evangelical, fundamentalist Christianity in America.

As the Constitution was in the process of ratification, a great groundswell of popular opinion demanded the addition of the Bill of Rights, the first ten amendments to the original Constitution. The First Amendment forbade the newly created federal government from establishing a religion through a government-supported national church and from infringing on religious freedom.

Christians were among the main advocates of adding the First Amendment to the original Constitution. And the same evangelical, fundamentalist religious forces led the struggle for separation of church and state, as well as religious freedom on the state level, particularly in Virginia and Massachusetts.

The First Amendment was thus no plot of atheistic conspirators, but the result of persevering Christians.

Thomas Jefferson presented his famous opinion that the First Amendment created a "wall of separation" between church and state in America in a letter he wrote to a group of fundamentalist Baptists in Connecticut—men who were part of the "Great Awakening" revival tradition in America. He told these Baptists exactly what they wanted to hear!

When the famous French historian and philosopher Alexis de Tocqueville visited America in the 1830s, he was struck by the deeply religious character of the country. He asked people from many different groups why religion was so strong in America. The answer surprised him:

> . . . they all attributed the peaceful dominion of religion in their country mainly to the separation of church and state. . . . I did not meet a single individual, of the clergy or the laity, who was not of the same opinion on this point.[4]

Today, some fear the prospect of religious revival as a threat to separation of church and state. History suggests otherwise. Thanks to the Great Awakening, separation of church and state, far from being an anti-Christian principle in origin, became, in fact, *the* Christian position on the subject.

5 ★ LIBERTY AND EQUALITY

As a movement, the Great Awakening reached the masses of men.

Driven by the conviction that all men are worthy to hear the Word of God, preachers such as Jonathan Edwards and George Whitefield sought to reach as many people as possible with the news of salvation.

These Great Awakening preachers also told the American people over and over: Every man is a creation of God, who also endowed them with rights and responsibilities. In God's eyes, all men are free and equal.

When the authors of the Declaration of Independence wrote that all men are created equal and are endowed by their Creator with certain inalienable rights, it was not, as Thomas Jefferson pointed out, "to find new principles, or new arguments never thought of." It was to declare to the world what were to Americans "self-evident truths."

Thanks to the Great Awakening, liberty and equality were for Americans not mere abstractions of the intellect.

They were convictions of the heart.

6 ★ ONE NATION UNDER GOD

It was not until 1954 that the words *under God* were added to our Pledge of Allegiance. But certainly Americans had long before thought of their country in that way—as a nation under God.

The Great Awakening substantially strengthened America's "sense of identity." It was an *American* phenomenon, for God recognized no regional boundaries as His Spirit moved across the land.

It was during the Great Awakening that the *idea of American union* was born—a body of people united not so much by common nationality or language or custom as by common conviction, a body of people united by belief in God and bonded together spiritually.

Americans were becoming one in heart, one in mind, one in striving for the same great spiritual and moral goals.

What God had joined together during the Great Awakening, no man, no movement, no civil war, no foreign foe has yet succeeded in sundering.

7 ★ DESTINY AND MISSION

==People who lived through the Great Awakening experienced what they believed to be a visitation from God.== God became a reality not only "up above" in heaven, but also "down below," in *this* world.

It was no longer possible to neatly divide life into the "sacred" and the "secular." God could be sensed working out His will for men and nations. And history became, in the minds of Americans, *His* story.

A powerful and positive vision of the future opened up. It held:

A sense of American destiny . . .

Consciousness of America's role in a divine design for liberating the earth . . .

The belief that God wanted to use America to launch world evangelization in the "latter days" of the earth . . .

Commitment to a mission sure to be accomplished, as long as Americans followed God's plans and purposes and joined in with His work of advancing the freedom of the world and the salvation of men.

"It is fit that mankind should be somewhat informed of God's design in the government of the world," wrote Jonathan Edwards, "because they are made capable of falling in with that design, of promoting it, and acting . . . as his friends and subjects."[5]

Edwards was a giant of the intellect—a great preacher, a great theologian, and America's greatest philosopher. Yet the truths he expressed, especially his philosophy of history, were not above the common man. They were clear and simple maxims that the ordinary people of America could grasp and use to make sense of the world.

"Providence is like a mighty wheel," declared Edwards, "whose circumference is so high that it is dreadful, with the glory of the God of Israel upon it."[6]

Thanks to the Great Awakening, the Providence of God became for Americans as real as the sights and sounds of the sensible world.

And history became a story writ by the very finger of God.

8 ★ THE REAL AMERICAN REVOLUTION

"What do we mean by the American Revolution?" asked John Adams. "Do we mean the American war?" No, he answered, "the Revolution was effected before the war commenced." Indeed, "the Revolution was in the hearts and minds of the people.... This radical change in the principles, opinions, sentiments, and affections of the people was the real American Revolution."[7]

The revival of religion was the real American Revolution!

The phenomenon of religious revival has made a great impression on many thoughtful Americans throughout our nation's history. Even people of quite different political persuasions have expressed their belief in the power of spiritual renewal.

Conservative Calvin Coolidge, who believed that America was born in a revival of religion, wrote:

It is of a great deal of significance that the generation which fought the American Revolution had been through a very extensive religious revival. They had heard the preaching of Jonathan Edwards. They had seen the revival meetings that were inspired also by the preaching of Whitefield. The religious experiences of those days made a profound impression upon the great body of the people. They made new thoughts and created new interests. They freed the public mind, through a deeper knowledge and more serious contemplation of the truth.[8]

Yet none other than Mr. Liberal himself, Franklin Delano Roosevelt, also said, "I doubt if there is any problem—social, political, or economic—that will not melt before the fire of spiritual awakening."[9]

Creating a common core of culture within all our diversity, the Great Awakening laid the foundations for morality in America. Firm convictions about matters of right and justice were forged in hearts and minds. A rock-solid ethical basis for democracy was put into place. A coalition of basic belief cut across section, class, denomination, and ideology.

Americans could "make a chain" (Ezekiel 7:23) as the need arose. They could stand together—through the Revolution, the ratification of the Constitution, the adoption of the Bill of Rights, and would, in this century, hold firm through two world wars.

Thanks to God and the Great Awakening, a consensus emerged—America's *original* "moral majority."

A national commitment to righteousness and to the moral foundations of democracy became so strong that even today it remains a source of hope for all mankind—a springboard for faith so that, as Lincoln said at Gettysburg, "This nation shall have a new birth of freedom—and that government of the people, by the people, for the people shall not perish from the earth."

PART TWO

THE RELIGION OF REVOLUTION

Resistance to tyrants is obedience to God.[1]
Thomas Jefferson

9 ★ THE TRUE PERMANENT REVOLUTION

In 1905, Leon Trotsky, a Russian communist revolutionary, coined the phrase *"permanent revolution."* He believed that a communist revolution in Russia would be only the beginning of a permanent process of radical change. Russian society, he hoped, would be transformed from top to bottom. He assumed that revolution in Russia would immediately spark simultaneous revolutions in the industrialized countries of Europe, and eventually all over the world.

In 1917, communism did triumph in Russia. The Bolshevik Party, with Lenin as the head, solidified its power.

After Lenin's death, Trotsky fought with Joseph Stalin over who would inherit Lenin's mantle. In opposition to Trotsky's slogan *"permanent revolution,"* Stalin advocated "socialism in one country."

Trotsky lost the succession struggle, but we must

not be misled by Stalin's slogan. This man who became one of history's most ruthless dictators aimed at world domination. He looked forward to the day when Soviet Russia, strengthened as a bastion of military power, could foment communist revolutions all over the globe.

In the minds of many twentieth-century people, communism has been associated with the cause of revolution. We have allowed the Fidel Castros, the Che Guevaras, and the Ho Chi Minhs to play the role of "freedom fighters" and "national liberators," to make army fatigues high fashion, to claim the mystique, the romance of revolution. With such unholy mixtures of Marxism and Christianity as evidenced by the "liberation theology" so popular in the Third World today, atheistic communism has even concocted a kind of "religion of revolution"!

Yet it is the American Revolution, *not the Russian Revolution, that is the* true *"permanent revolution."*

Ours has not been merely a revolution in one country, or in one time. The American Revolution has influenced the whole course of modern history.

It was the inspiration for the French Revolution of 1789. Unlike ours, the French Revolution went to extremes of terror and tyranny. But it did initiate a process of progress toward democracy in all of Western Europe.

Who would wish to turn the clock back to the *ancien regime*, to the way things were in Europe before 1789, before the French Revolution, during the age of absolute monarchy and the divine right of kings?

The political landscape of Western Europe today

is dominated by democracies. The common man enjoys personal liberties and a standard of living that would have been the envy of medieval kings! Yet just two centuries ago, the average person in Europe was born a serf, lived and died a serf, with no hope of anything better for his children.

The Spirit that the American Revolution unleashed has never died. The revolution that began in 1776 is still at work, here and abroad.

With the liberation of the slaves and the extension of civil rights to all, we have perfected the principles of that revolution at home.

Around the world today, the principles for which we fought in 1776 are still causes for which men lay down their lives. The issues that led us to declare independence are the issues now in Poland, in Afghanistan, and in the vast Soviet empire in Europe and Asia.

"Resistance to tyrants is obedience to God," wrote Thomas Jefferson.[2] Such was the spirit of the American Revolution. Such is the real "religion of revolution."

And the tyrants of the world still tremble before this holy truth!

10 ★ ROOTED IN RELIGIOUS CONVICTIONS

Today, few understand the truths of the Declaration of Independence. Some openly reject the ideas of the Declaration in favor of such alien ideologies as Marxism, existentialism, and humanism. Others dare to say: There are no "self-evident truths" at all, and it is from our wants and passions—not from the "Laws of Nature and Nature's God"—that individual rights are derived.

Skepticism and cynicism have set in. Certain historians and their pupils—some of whom are the teachers of our children—proclaim that the Founding Fathers covered up narrow, selfish goals with high-sounding words. Gresham Machen, one of this century's greatest religious scholars, decried this trend as early as 1931:

No principle, they are telling us, was involved in the American Revolution; economic causes alone produced that struggle; and Patrick Henry was indulging in cheap melodrama when he said: "Give me liberty or give me death."[3]

Here lies the root of our sense of purposelessness as a nation today. If the truths of the Declaration of Independence are not really truths . . .

If there are no principles, only passions—no convictions, only wishes . . .

If the "Laws of Nature and Nature's God" are but a myth . . .

If there is no will of God, no law of God for men and civilization . . .

Then the notion of a national purpose and destiny makes no sense.

If there is no God who assigns purposes and decides destinies for men and nations, then there is only what we as human beings assign and decide.

What our generation needs to understand is that the Declaration of Independence is a document that states spiritual concepts. Equality, liberty, the rights of man, government by the consent of the governed—we cannot see and touch these things. They are ideals rooted in religious convictions.

Thomas Jefferson, principal author of the Declaration of Independence, noted that the Declaration did not aim at "originality of principle," but was intended to be "an expression of the American mind." It rested upon the "harmonizing sentiments of the day."

It is no mere coincidence that the Great Awakening, which occurred on the eve of the American Revolution, deeply influenced "the American mind." The "revolution in religion" led to the "religion of revolution"—the religious consensus affirmed in the Declaration of Independence and around which the American people rallied during the Revolution.

11 ★ THE LAWS OF NATURE AND NATURE'S GOD

The very first paragraph of the Declaration of Independence uses the phrase "the Laws of Nature and Nature's God":

When, in the course of human events, it becomes necessary for one people to dissolve the political bands which have connected them with another, and to assume, among the Powers of the earth, the separate and equal station to which the Laws of Nature and Nature's God entitle them, a decent respect to the opinions of mankind requires that they should declare the causes which impel them to separation.

All the basic concepts of the Declaration of Independence were very familiar to the Americans of that time. But what was then "an expression of the American mind" no longer seems obvious to many Americans today. We especially find it difficult to understand what eighteenth-century Americans meant by the "Laws of Nature and Nature's God." Yet the whole Declaration—the basic document of the American political tradition—rests squarely on that concept!

American political thought of the eighteenth century was thoroughly imbued with the ideas developed by English philosopher John Locke in his *Second Treatise of Civil Government.* Locke repeatedly employed such phrases as "law of nature," "natural law," and "natural rights." The same "inalienable rights" of which the Declaration speaks were also posited in the *Second Treatise.* It is to that source that we must go to find what eighteenth-century Americans meant by "the Laws of Nature and Nature's God."

Here is how Locke defined the "law of nature": ". . . Reason, which is that law, teaches all mankind who will but consult it that, being all equal and independent, no one ought to harm another in his life, health, liberty and possessions. . . ."[4]

"Reason, which is that law," or the "law of nature"—that is a definition that surprises us. Did our Founding Fathers, and most Americans of the eighteenth century, believe that the "Laws of Nature and Nature's God" are *reason,* human reason?

Yes, indeed they did. But we are apt to make serious mistakes in interpreting their principles, unless we remember several vital points.

In the first place, our Founding Fathers believed that any truth found by human reason is something man *discovers,* not something he makes up or creates. They did not think that man makes or creates his own "truth."

In the second place, our Founding Fathers did not think that man is by nature good, and they did not overestimate the power of human reason acting alone.

Locke himself recognized how limited human reason is. He gave this explanation of why human reason alone cannot find all the truths of "the Laws of Nature and Nature's God":

'Tis too hard a task for unassisted Reason, to establish Morality in all its parts upon its true foundations, with a clear and convincing Light. And 'tis at least a surer and shorter Way, to the Apprehension of the . . . mass of Mankind, that one manifestly sent from God . . . tell them their Duties; and require their obedience; than leave it to the long, and sometimes intricate Deductions of Reason, to be made out to them. . . . And the reason of it is not hard to be found in Men's Necessities, Passions, Vices, and mistaken Interests, which turn their Thoughts another way. . . . And he that shall collect all the moral Rules of the Philosophers, and compare them with those contained in the New Testament, will find them to come short of the Morality delivered by our Saviour, and taught by his Apostles, a College made up for the most part of ignorant, but inspired Fishermen.

Such a Law of Morality Jesus Christ hath given us in the New Testament . . . by Revelation. We have from him a full and sufficient Rule for our direction, and comformable to that of Reason. But the truth and obligation of its Precepts have their force, and are put past doubt to us, by the evidence of his Mission. He was sent by God: His miracles show it; and the authority of God in his Precepts cannot be questioned. Here Morality has a sure Standard, that Revelation vouches, and Reason cannot gainsay, nor question; but both together witness to come from God the great Law maker. And such an one as this out of the New Testament, I think the World never had, nor can anyone say is anywhere else to be found. . . .[5]

Religion played a major role in Locke's moral and political philosophy. His reasoning about the "Laws of Nature and Nature's God" rested squarely upon the religious principle that man was created by God:

"No one ought to harm another in his life, health, liberty, or possessions; for men being all the workmanship of one omnipotent and infinitely wise Maker—all the servants of one sovereign master, sent into the world by his order, and about his business—they are his property whose workmanship they are, made to last during his, not one another's, pleasure. . . ."[6]

Perhaps the two most important concepts in our Declaration of Independence so influenced by Locke are creature and Creator. Without them, the Declaration's "self-evident" truths crumble!

12 ★ THE AMERICAN CIVIL RELIGION

Our "religion of revolution" expressed in the spiritual concepts of the Declaration of Independence does not violate separation of church and state. Neither does it threaten our pluralistic society.

America has never been a "Christian nation." Our government is not a "Christian republic"—no counterpart to the "Islamic republic" of the Ayatollah Khomeini. Rather, America is a pluralistic nation, with separation of church and state and religious liberty for all. Each citizen may worship God as he pleases, or even profess atheism.

Yet we remain a "nation under God." Even today, 95 percent of Americans profess a belief in God. We always have as a nation. There is no reason why this consensus of opinion should threaten separation of church and state, religious liberty, or pluralism.

To understand American religious belief, it is necessary to distinguish between two kinds of religion.

The first is the *religion of the individual.* At issue is the individual's personal salvation and his future life. This is the religion of our churches—the religion of our diverse denominations and many sects.

The second kind of religion is the *religion of the citizen and the nation*—what some have called the "American civil religion."[7] At issue is the destiny of America as a nation, a nation conscious of the "Laws of Nature and Nature's God." It is what we have called the "religion of revolution," and its fundamental doctrines are stated in the Declaration of Independence.

Religious liberty and separation of church and state make personal religious belief of the first kind (concerning personal salvation and the future life) strictly a private matter. But at the same time, the great majority of Americans share some basic elements of a common religious orientation. Such a commonality of religious belief is no threat to separation of church and state, because religious liberty has been a "sacred tenet" of sorts of the American civil religion!

13 ★ THE DOCTRINES OF DEMOCRACY

The Declaration of Independence is the great sacred document of the American civil religion. To call it sacred is not to suggest that it was directly "inspired" by God as the Bible was.

However, the Declaration does contain certain absolute ("self-evident") truths that are *doctrines of democracy:*

Equality of rights . . .
Liberty for all . . .
Limited government . . .
Government by consent of the governed . . .
The right of revolution. . . .

While the Great Awakening prepared the hearts and minds of the people for the American Revolution, it will take another "revolution in religion" in our day to renew our "religion of revolution."

The greatest challenge of contemporary American culture and politics is to restore the Spirit of 1776, to renew the promise and the ideals of that revolution.

Part of that challenge entails understanding anew the theory—indeed the theology—that justified it. It was that theory—that religion—that made America different, that made America . . . America.

Without that theory, without that vision, America will perish.

PART THREE

MINE EYES HAVE SEEN THE GLORY

*Mine eyes have seen the glory
of the coming of the Lord.*
"The Battle Hymn of the Republic"

14 ★ "THE BATTLE HYMN OF THE REPUBLIC"

Mine eyes have seen the glory of the coming of the Lord;
He is trampling out the vintage where the grapes of wrath are stored;
He hath loosed the fateful lightning of His terrible swift sword,
His truth is marching on.

These words from "The Battle Hymn of the Republic" ring out on many occasions today. Like our national anthem, it is a song for all seasons.

But it was written literally as a "battle hymn"—in 1862, during the Civil War. Stanza two especially seems to be a description of conditions in the Union army camps:

I have seen Him in the watch-fires of a hundred circling camps;

*They have builded Him an altar in the evening dews
   and damps;
I can read His righteous sentence by the dim of flaring
   lamps,
His day is marching on.*

Yet clearly the "Battle Hymn" envisions more than a mere sectional struggle or regional division.

Stanzas three and four cast the Civil War in the perspective of eternity. They relate the moral cause over which the Blue and Gray fought to the high themes of salvation, redemption, and judgment:

*I have read a fiery gospel, writ in burnish'd rows of steel:
As ye deal with My contemners, so with you My grace
   shall deal,
Let the Hero, born of woman, crush the serpent with His
   heel,
Since God is marching on.*

*He has sounded forth the trumpet that shall never call
   retreat;
He is sifting out the hearts of men before His judgment
   seat;
Oh, be swift, my soul, to answer Him!
Be jubilant, my feet!
Our God is marching on.*

Today such epic language and literary grandeur seem almost embarrassing. We are afraid of being thought jingoists or being accused of mixing religion with politics.

Safely tranquilized, the American Spirit slumbers. Leave apocalyptic struggle to George Lucas and Steven Spielberg, we think. Let them entertain the kids with it.

"The Battle Hymn of the Republic" breaks all the rules of contemporary public life in America:

It is super patriotic . . .

It is extravagantly optimistic.

Without shame, it linked our country's causes with the plans of God. Yet it unquestionably captured the mood of many in that less timid age, the nineteenth century, the era of the slogan "Manifest Destiny."

The Civil War, like the Abolitionist Movement that led to it, was part of a broader fight for progress evidenced in a struggle for social, racial, religious, economic, and political reform; and a fight for improved working conditions, prison reform, better care for the mentally ill, expanded educational opportunity, women's rights, a more open political process, and so on.

When the streams of American history converged in the nineteenth century, the revolutionary religion of the Great Awakening and the "religion of revolution" from the American Revolution, came together to form a rushing torrent. A tidal wave would sweep across the continent and even beyond, or so it was believed. Even the most sober and serious expected that the world was going to be evangelized. There was the hope that millions of souls would be converted and would, in turn, transform human society, building a new world civilization based on democracy and human rights.

It seemed that the world was being prepared for the ultimate destiny of all history.

15 ★ AN IRRESISTIBLE REVOLUTION

As the curtain went up on the nineteenth century, the drama of history was building to a climax. Mankind was poised to play the heroic role for which such milestones of liberation as the American Revolution had prepared the way. The scene was set for unprecedented progress, giant leaps in politics, economics, science—in every field of human endeavor.

On the world stage stood a new actor—the United States of America. In the achievement of freedom and the realization of the dreams of all past generations of mankind, America had already performed magnificently.

During 1831 and 1832, Alexis de Tocqueville, the great French philosopher and historian, visited America to view this spectacular story from a front-row seat. This profound critic of the trends of modern history was not disappointed in what he saw. "It was there that civilized man was destined to build society on new foundations," he wrote, "for the first time applying theories till then unknown or deemed unworkable, to present the world with a spectacle for which past history has not prepared it."[1]

In the last two hundred years or so, many nations have aspired to build on the same foundations as America and to apply its same theories. Even now, that drama unfolds—sometimes with tragedy, but sometimes with a success that makes our spirits soar.

Today, as never before, when this great experiment in civilization seems threatened even in America, it is vital that we understand the forces that drove America—with the world on its coattails—to such heights.

When de Tocqueville visited America in the 1830s, he brought with him a profound conviction held with "a kind of religious awe," that an "irresistible revolution" had been advancing "for centuries in spite of every obstacle."

The "irresistible revolution" was the "gradual and progressive development of social equality," which de Tocqueville identified as the essence of democracy:

It was not necessary that God himself should speak in order that we may discover the unquestionable signs of his will. It is enough to ascertain what is the habitual course of nature and the constant tendency of events. I know, without special revelation, that the planets move in the orbits traced by the Creator's hand.

If the men of our time should be convinced, by attentive

observation and sincere reflection, that the gradual and progressive development of social equality is at once the past and the future of their history, this discovery alone would confer upon the change the sacred character of a divine decree. To attempt to check democracy would be in that case to resist the will of God; and the nations would then be constrained to make the best of the social lot awarded to them by Providence.[2]

De Tocqueville recognized that democracy, for all its benefits and virtues, also carried certain disadvantages and vices. He had seen the problems of democracy and the "irresistible revolution" of modern times most violently displayed in his native France, where the revolution had gone on a tangent of terror.

In his great work *Democracy in America,* de Tocqueville sought to teach the lessons on democracy that he had learned in America:

I confess that in America I saw more than America; I sought there the image of democracy itself, with its inclinations, its character, its prejudices, and its passions, in order to learn what we have to fear or to hope from its progress.[3]

De Tocqueville came to America to study politics, but he was in for a surprise:

On my arrival in the United States the religious aspect of the country was the first thing that struck my attention; and the longer I stayed there, the more I perceived the great political consequences resulting from this new state of things.[4]

In much of Europe, the forces pushing for progress toward democracy were at odds with the dominant, state-established, government-controlled churches. Religion was tied to the "Old Regime"—autocracy, privilege, and feudalism. The "spirit of religion and the spirit of freedom" marched "in opposite directions." But in America, observed de Tocqueville, these spirits "were intimately united," reigning "in common over the same country."[5]

De Tocqueville had come to America to study the most democratic country in the world, but he also found the secret to America's success as a democracy—its distinction of being the most religious nation. He wrote:

. . . There is no country in the world where the Christian religion retains a greater influence over the souls of men than in America; and there can be no greater proof of its utility and conformity to human nature than that its influence is powerfully felt over the most enlightened and free nation of the earth.[6]

Some students of the history of religion see the First Amendment, which forbids Congress from making any law establishing religion or infringing upon religious freedom, as the beginning of the end of Christian influence on American civilization. They repeat the error of the old Puritans of the Massachusetts Bay Colony—and so many Christians before, Catholic and Protestant alike—by imagining that religion is strengthened by government support and weakened by separation of church and state.

The truth is just the opposite.

De Tocqueville, seeking am explanation for the strength of religion as well as the strength of democracy in America, questioned representatives of many religious denominations and sects. He received a paradoxical answer. We have already quoted it, but it is worth repeating:

> *. . . They all attributed the peaceful dominion of religion in their country mainly to separation of church and state. I do not hesitate to confirm that during my stay in America I did not meet a single individual, of the clergy or the laity, who was not of the same opinion on this point.*[7]

De Tocqueville concluded that separation of church and state *strengthened* both religion and democracy in America.

As de Tocqueville listened to Americans speak, he discovered the connection between democracy and religion:

> *Religion in America takes no direct part in the government of society, but it must be regarded as the first of their political institutions; for if it does not impart a taste for freedom, it facilitates the use of it. Indeed, it is this same point of view that the inhabitants of the United States themselves look upon religious belief. I do not know whether all Americans have a sincere faith in their religion—for who can search the human heart?—but I am certain that they hold it to be indispensable to the maintenance of republican institutions. This opinion is not peculiar to a class of citizens or to a party, but it belongs to the whole nation and to every rank of society.*[8]

One of the first American history school textbooks was published in 1832, the very time of de Tocqueville's visit. Written by Noah Webster of the "blue-backed speller" fame, it confirms the Frenchman's observations. Generations of students in one-room schoolhouses would learn this as the "origin of civil liberty":

Almost all the civil liberty now enjoyed in the world owes its origin to the principles of the Christian religion. Men began to understand their natural rights . . . and civil liberty has been gradually advancing . . . as genuine Christianity has prevailed. By the principles of the Christian religion we are not to understand the decisions of ecclesiastical councils . . . nor . . . any particular church established by law. . . . No, the religion which has introduced civil liberty, is the religion of Christ and his apostles which enjoins humility, piety, and benevolence; which acknowledges in every person a brother, or a sister, and a citizen with equal rights. This is genuine Christianity, and to this we owe our free . . . government.[9]

16 ★ THE DEVIL'S TIME IS NEARLY OUT

By the beginning of the nineteenth century, the triumph of absolute religious liberty in America proved to be one of the great victories of all time for Christianity. One American after another testified to de Tocqueville that separation of church and state *strengthens* religion, and the nineteenth century bears this out.

Having separation of church and state—with no governmental coercion or constraint, financial or otherwise—men could understand very clearly the essence of true religion. It is a matter of free heart belief, and a forced religion is no religion at all.

With government out of the business of forcing religion on nonbelievers, persuasion and reason became the only proper—indeed the only rational—human means for the conversion of souls. And thanks to the First Amendment and similar provisions for the freedom of religion at the state and local level, men of denominations who a century earlier might have been jailed for their beliefs (the Baptists being a good case in point) were now free to disciple their neighbors—whether next door or on the other side of the world.

Nineteenth-century America was a place of great religious foment. Many new religious movements appeared. But it was traditional Christianity—evangelical and Bible-believing—that most prospered. Christians set out with the goal of nothing less than reaching the world for Christ in one generation, and they very nearly succeeded!

The nineteenth century saw such a surge in Christian growth that it is called the "great century" of evangelism. "Because of a combination of geographic expansion, inner vitality, and the effect upon mankind as a whole," concluded Kenneth Scott Latourette, the late Yale scholar of church history, the nineteenth century "constituted the greatest century which Christianity had thus far known."[10]

With the United States as launching pad, world missions proceeded on an unprecedented scale, and with unprecedented results. A network of mission stations covered the earth. The Bible circulated in many hundreds of languages and dialects. By the end of the century, there was hardly a country in the world where missionaries had not gone or the Bible was not available.

In America itself, evangelism reached new peaks. At mass crusades, people gathered in record-breaking numbers.

As the nineteenth century ended, the buoyant optimism of Christians of that age spilled over into the twentieth century. On the eve of World War I, B.H. Carroll, a Texas Baptist preacher and founder and first president of Southwestern, the largest seminary in the world, wrote: ". . . All the kingdoms of this world [will] become the kingdom of our Lord and Christ. And it is not so very far off. . . ."[11]

Typical of the Christians of that time, Carroll practically hung onto the edge of his seat as the stage was set, so he believed, for the great climax of history:

The devil's time is nearly out; events are moving rapidly; ocean and air are navigated; telegraph wires long rusted with commercial and political lies shall shine with the transmission of messages of mercy and salvation. . . .

All the earth swept with revival power from continent to continent. . . . [12]

17 ★ DOERS OF THE WORD

In nineteenth-century America, religion was not consigned to a corner of the world, content with a round of motions and mutters, afraid to go forth and challenge culture and civilization. Religion established the very foundation of civilization.

It was a time when large numbers were, as the Bible puts it, "doers of the word and not hearers only" (James 1:22, *King James Version*). Men knew that, "Pure religion and undefiled before God . . . is this, To visit the fatherless and widows . . ." (James 1:27, *King James Version*). Their duty was to fulfill "the royal law according to the Scriptures, thou shalt love thy neighbor as thyself."

The world had never seen such disinterested benevolence, such selfless charity as burst forth in the nineteenth century. Never before had so many done so much for so many. And the only compulsion was the gentle prodding of divine love for all mankind.

Toward the end of the nineteenth century, something called the "Social Gospel" appeared. Some apostles of the new creed preached a message of benevolence to society somewhat severed from the "Ye must be born again" message of traditional Christianity.

In fact, evangelical Christianity was already acutely socially conscious, and could scarcely have been more so. Salvation was not the objective of all the good works of nineteenth-century Christianity: the reigning doctrine was salvation by grace through faith and "not of works, lest any man should boast" (Ephesians 2:9, *King James Version*). Nevertheless, good works were thought to be the *fruit* of salvation. As the New Testament declares, "As the body without the spirit is dead, so faith without works is dead also" (James 2:26, *King James Version*).

Anthony Ashley Cooper, Earl of Shaftesbury, the greatest English Christian reformer of the nineteenth century, spoke for evangelicals in America as well as in England when he told a gathering of social service workers in 1859:

"When people say we should think more of the soul and less of the body, my answer is that the same God who made the soul made the body also. . . . I maintain that God is worshipped not only by the spiritual but by the material creation. Our bodies, the temples of the Holy Ghost, ought not to be corrupted by preventable disease, degraded by avoidable filth, and disabled for his service by unnecessary suffering.[13]

It was no preacher of a mere social gospel but Charles Grandison Finney himself, the founding father of mass city-wide revival crusades and a firm fundamentalist, who, declaring that sin is selfishness and virtue selflessness, preached that each Christian should "have the determination at being useful in the highest degree possible."[14]

Nineteenth-century Christians did not view benevolence as a substitute for evangelism, or evangelism as a substitute for benevolence. In the religious vision of Christianity's greatest century, evangelism and benevolence were two sides of the same coin. As *The Christian Spectator* declared in 1832, "Piety grows by the operations of benevolence, and the operations of benevolence acquire new strength by the growth of piety."

Missionaries were preachers and "Peace Corps" workers rolled into one! One missionary phrased the purpose of missions this way:

The object for which the missionaries felt themselves impelled . . . was to honor God, by making known his will, and to benefit those heathen tribes by making them acquainted with the Christian way of life; to turn them from their follies and crimes, idolatries and oppressions, to the service and enjoyment of the living God and adorable Redeemer; to give them the Bible in their own tongue, with ability to read it for themselves; to introduce and extend among them the more useful arts and usages of civilized and Christianized society.[15]

Wherever Christianity was proclaimed, it tended eventually but effectively to cease cruel entertainments (as it did the gladiator fights in Rome), to abolish slavery, to overthrow tyranny.

It condemned parricide, infanticide, genocide

It declared true principles of individual liberty and equated true morality with true freedom.

It revealed the just and legitimate foundations of government—the consent of the people and the inalienable rights of man.

In the nineteenth century, Christianity was the vital driving force, the powerful inner dynamo of American civilization.

The task at hand seemed to be nothing less than the transformation of Planet Earth in accordance with what were believed to be the goals of God—a coming age of peace and freedom not only for America but for all mankind.

18 ★ FROM PHILANTHROPY TO POLITICS

What were the means by which nineteenth-century American Christians hoped to usher in a new age?

For evangelical Christians, of course, evangelism and missions held the key. Society could be transformed only if men could be transformed. And the basic tenet of evangelicalism was the necessity of the "new birth." The born-again would literally have new natures.

But the "new birth" was believed to be only the beginning. Following it came new life, with new perspectives and new motives. A driving inclination to universal benevolence would characterize the truly converted.

Thus, in the fruits of salvation—determination to usefulness, holiness, and sanctification—lay the impact on society. Piety strengthened by benevolence and benevolence strengthened by piety could revolutionize the world.

And how would born-again people express their benevolence?

First, through philanthropy:

By aiding the poor and disadvantaged through such private voluntary collective efforts as the Young Men's Christian Association (YMCA), the Red Cross, and the Salvation Army . . .

By establishing organizations (or using existing denominational ones) to build and operate hospitals, orphanages, settlement houses, and schools and colleges . . .

By working through conventional evangelistic and missionary groups such as the American Bible Society and the American Tract Society, which made service to the body, as well as salvation of the soul, their business.

By mid-century, an incredible number of voluntary philanthropic societies had sprung up in America. One minister listed them:

Missionary societies, tract societies, education societies, moral societies, and other societies of various names for the purpose of feeding the hungry, clothing the naked, instructing the ignorant, saving the lost, and promoting peace on earth and mutual amity among mankind.[16]

In such associations and organized ministries, reformers had a powerful tool. Individuals could do jointly what they could not do alone. Feelings and interests roused through associations became a creative principle that called forth new forces. The result was expansion of the individual's consciousness of his power to do good to all mankind and to make a difference in the world.

Religion made social reform imperative. It held that since social evils resulted from individual sin and selfishness, progress would come by first reforming individuals through conversion. From regeneration of the soul, regeneration of society would follow.

The first priority of the would-be Christian reformer, then, was conversion—from which philanthropy would follow.

But there were also other means of showing benevolence. As the century wore on, political action with the goal of social reform became increasingly important. According to historian Russell Nye, "Reform in the United States received its most powerful support from religious evangelism...."[17] In fact,

The connections between evangelism and reform were quickly noted by the socially conservative. Revivalists and their followers tended to get mixed up with unsettling matters like abolitionism, women's rights, and prohibition. Nonetheless, the opposition was simply buried by evangelism's sweep across the nineteenth century.[18]

In pursuit of their goals, nineteenth-century Christians inevitably turned to politics. "The church must take right ground in regard to politics," preached evangelist Charles G. Finney, who added that:

... The time has come that Christians must vote for honest men, and take consistent ground in politics.... They must let the world see that the church will uphold no man in office who is known to be a knave, or

an adulterer. . . . If he will give his vote only for honest men, the country will be obliged to have upright rulers. All parties will be compelled to put up honest men as candidates. . . . As on the subjects of slavery and temperance, so on this subject, the church must act right, or the country will be ruined. . . .[19]

Perhaps anticipating charges of violating the Constitutional tenet of separation of church and state, Finney proclaimed: "Politics are a part of religion in such a country as this, and Christians must do their duty to the country as a part of their duty to God."[20]

And do their duty they did!

Nearly all major reform movements that began in the nineteenth century, mostly at the instigation of Christians, eventually succeeded in one way or another. Some of the victories were rolled back. For example, the Eighteenth Amendment passed in 1919 to establish prohibition was repealed by the Twenty-first in 1933.

But the Nineteenth Amendment guaranteeing women's suffrage was *not* repealed. And most of the other reform movements, such as prison, education, poor relief, made a permanent impact on American society.

Some of the planks in the platform of nineteenth-century religious reform are difficult to understand from a contemporary perspective. Measures such as temperance and Sabbath sanctity strike us as efforts to use law to force religion down the throats of unbelievers.

Admittedly, nineteenth-century Christians derived their principles from the Bible as they understood it. But they also articulated "secular" arguments for their positions, arguments designed to appeal to all rational and reasonable men of whatever religious persuasion.

The evangelicals believed that temperance, for example, while in their opinion taught by the Bible, could also be defended as necessary for the progress of civilization. Alcohol was seen as the chief obstacle to the physical, social, and moral health of the nation. In light of the terrible consequences that alcohol and other drugs are having on contemporary American society, who would say that the temperance-promoters were entirely wrong?

As for Sabbath observance and laws prohibiting the conducting of business as usual on Sunday, they, too, could be justified with more than proof texts from the Bible. "The intensity of the nineteenth-century drive to maintain the observance of a strict Christian Sabbath," comments historian Robert Handy, "comes as a surprise to many twentieth-century Americans, but it was then seen as an important sign of evangelical advance."[21]

Religion was necessary for morality, so the reasoning went, and churches were necessary for religion. It followed that if Sabbath observance was necessary for the churches (because if the work of the world went on on Sundays, Christians would have to participate and hence be absent from the pew), then society had a compelling interest in keeping Sunday special.

Thus American Methodists resolved in 1844, concerning Sabbath observance:

. . . Were this precept blotted from the decalogue, and men left without the restraints which it imposes, religion (and of course morality) would cease to exert their saving and hallowed influences.[22]

Similarly, American Presbyterians in 1818 argued that because men and society need a regular break in activity, Sabbath observance is a good civil practice, too:

The Lord's Day, viewed in a political light entirely, affords so many benefits calculated for the promotion of present enjoyment in all the relations of life, as to claim for it the veneration and homage of sound statesmen.[23]

From philanthropy to politics, Christians stood ready to use whatever means necessary and consistent with their goals.

Some were even prepared for war, if it were the only effective means to rid society of certain evils, as proved to be the case with slavery.

19 ★ LET US DIE TO MAKE MEN FREE

Slavery, of course, was an issue that divided American Christians along regional lines. And after about 1830, Southern Christians did indeed use the Bible to rationalize their support of slavery.

When war came, Southern Christians identified God, morality, and historical destiny with slavery, the Confederacy, and the war. In 1864, for example, Southern Presbyterians declared their lack of hesitancy in affirming "that it is the peculiar mission of the Southern Church to conserve the institution of slavery, and to make it a blessing both to master and slave."[24]

To the end of the century, Southern Christians—and Southern Baptists in particular—refused to admit that either slavery or secession were morally or constitutionally wrong.

History, of course, was on the side of the Union and abolitionism; and in the minds of Northern

Christians, so was God. Northern Christians did not welcome war over the cause of slavery, but neither did they shrink from it when it came. It was common to identify the old theme of America's divine destiny with Northern success. An outspoken Methodist Bishop Gilbert Haven preached:

"To save this land to universal liberty and universal brotherhood, supported by universal law and sanctified by universal piety, is to save all lands. It may take all our sons, all our treasure, all our generation to destroy the enemy that is seeking to prevent this consummation."[25]

But following victory, predicted the Bishop, other nations will behold "the image of the transfigured Christ shining in our uplifted face, that will glow, like that of Moses, with the radiance of his divine countenance."[26]

Time has a way of healing many wounds. By century's end, Christians north and south were again united in a common vision of the future.

On the eve of a new war of apocalyptic dimensions—a war unlike any before in the history of the world—the closing stanza of the "Battle Hymn" could serve as the holy war march of a united republic:

In the beauty of the lilies
Christ was born across the sea,
With a glory in His bosom that transfigures you and me;
As He died to make men holy, let us die to make men free,
While God is marching on.

PART FOUR
OVER THERE!

*And we won't come back
till it's over, over there!*
George M. Cohan

20 ★ TO MAKE THE WORLD SAFE FOR DEMOCRACY

On April 2, 1917, Woodrow Wilson, the president of the United States, addressed Congress. "The world must be made safe for democracy . . ." he said. Then he broke the awesome news:

"It is a distressing and oppressive duty, Gentlemen of the Congress, which I have performed in thus addressing you. There are, it may be, many months of fiery trial and sacrifice ahead of us. It is a fearful thing to lead this great peaceful people into war, into the most terrible and disastrous of all wars, civilization itself seeming to be in the balance. But the right is more precious than peace, and we shall fight for the things which we have always carried nearest our hearts—for democracy, for the right of those who submit to authority to have a voice in their own governments, for the rights and liberties of small nations, for a universal dominion of right by such a concert of free peoples as shall bring peace and safety to all nations and

make the world itself at last free. . . . The day has come when America is privileged to spend her blood and her might for the principles that gave her birth. . . . God helping her, she can do no other."[1]

Four days later, on April 6, America entered World War I.

After reading the headlines on the morning of April 6, George M. Cohan wrote for the warrior republic a new "battle hymn," an even more celebrated American war song, one destined to become *the* song classic of World War I.

The chorus was done before Cohan entered his car for work:

Over there, over there,
Send the word, send the word over there,
That the Yanks are coming, the Yanks are coming,
The drums rum-tumming everywhere.
So prepare, say a prayer,
Send the word, send the word to beware,
We'll be over, we're coming over,
And we won't come back till
It's over, over there!

The verse was written before the car reached the Cohan & Harris offices in Manhattan:

Johnnie, get your gun, get your gun, get your gun,
Take it on the run, on the run, on the run;
Hear them calling you and me,
Every son of Liberty.
Hurry right away, no delay, go today.
Make your daddy glad

To have had such a lad,
Tell your sweetheart not to pine,
To be proud her boy's in line.

Cohan's friend Joe Humphreys, the famous ring announcer of Madison Square Garden and the first to hear the song, declared, "George, you've got a song."

So he had.

"Over There" swept the land. Within a month of publication, it could be heard in every corner of America—sung, hummed, whistled.

And so, over there, over there, America's youth went . . .

To the old world to make it new . . .

To fight the war to end all wars . . .

To make the world safe for democracy. . . .

21 ★ MANIFEST DESTINY

In his address to Congress calling for a declaration of war, Woodrow Wilson moved America from her past to her future.

Everything before pointed to this moment.

At nineteenth-century midpoint, the possibility of American intervention overseas for the cause of freedom had been hinted at. In 1853, an article in *The Presbyterian Quarterly* had suggested:

On the fields of Europe, among the rotten systems, reeking with lies and oppression, and in regions red with the blood of saints, the lines may be closed up, and we of the western world be forced to take sides. . . . The battle of Armageddon is yet to be fought.[2]

Had it been hinted at even before the Revolution—in John Adams' diary entry for February 1765? At that time, he wrote:

I always consider the settlement of America with reverence and wonder, as the opening of a grand scheme and design in Providence for the illumination of the ignorant, and the emancipation of the slavish part of mankind all over the earth.[3]

Certainly America's involvement in Europe in World War I—fighting for democracy, protecting freedom from aggression by autocratic powers, extending the dominion of human rights—was the natural extension of the nineteenth-century American concept of "Manifest Destiny"—the idea that God has assigned the American nation dominion over most of the continent.

Why was such a destiny so "manifest," so obvious to so many?

Because Americans believed that God is a friend of freedom, that God has decreed all men to be partakers of liberty, that it is therefore the divine moral duty of all men and nations to fight for the rights of humanity.

The "destiny" of the United States to expand westward—some even spoke of movement across the Pacific—was conceived as a mission to extend the principles of the universal rights of man to new territories.

William Gilpin, soldier, explorer, and governor of the Colorado Territory, made a classic statement of the full program of "Manifest Destiny" when he described America's yet untransacted destiny:

To subdue the continent—to rush over this vast field to the Pacific Ocean—to animate the many hundred millions of its people, and to cheer them upward—to set the principle of self-government at work—to establish a new order in human affairs—to set free the enslaved—to regenerate superannuated nations—to change darkness into light—to stir up the sleep of a hundred centuries—to teach old nations new civilization—to confirm the destiny of the human race—to carry the career of mankind to its culminating point—to cause stagnant people to be reborn—to perfect science—to emblazon history with the conquest of peace—to shed a new and resplendent glory upon mankind—to unite the world in one social family—to dissolve the spell of tyranny and exalt charity—to absolve the curse that weights down humanity and to shed blessings around the world.[4]

Was this "imperialism"—as some indeed charged during the Mexican-American War of 1848 and the Spanish-American War of 1898? If so, it was imperialism of a quite peculiar kind.

Is an empire of freedom really an empire in the usual sense? Certainly there was none like it before in the history of imperial politics.

And even those who charged "imperialism" in 1848 and 1898 used the same principles as their opponents. It was with a high sense of mission that Mark Twain, for example, attacked the war with Spain: "I pray you to pause and consider. Against our traditions we are now entering upon an unjust and trivial war, a war against a helpless people, and for a base object—robbery."[5]

The same nation Twain criticized, it should be pointed out, in 1946 freed the territory in question—the Philippines—and assisted it in developing its own democracy.

But whatever ambiguities or inconsistencies there were in 1848 and 1898, there seemed to be none in the war of 1914—the "Great War," or the "war to end all wars," or as we know it, World War I.

22 ★ THE VENGEFUL PROVIDENCE OF GOD

President Woodrow Wilson was wrong when he said that World War I would end all wars. Unfortunately, it also failed to make the world safe for democracy. This son of a Presbyterian minister, a deeply committed Christian himself, was wrong in thinking the battle won to have been Armageddon.

Wilson was right about one thing, however. Like it or not, admit it or not, the United States, he observed, has a divine task:

The stage is set, the destiny is disclosed. It has come about by no plan of our conceiving, but by the hand of God who led us unto this way. We cannot turn back. We can only go forward, with lifted eyes and freshened spirit, to follow the vision. It was of this that we dreamed at our birth.[6]

These words were given at the end of World War I.

Of course, the truth is that we can *try* to turn back, *try* to deny our destiny as a nation, but only at enormous cost. President Wilson predicted that if the United States attempted isolationism and shirked its duty in the world, the "vengeful Providence of God" would bring a new war in which many more Americans would die than had in World War I.

In World War I, 53,402 Americans died in battle.

In World War II, 291,557 Americans died in battle.

There were some legitimate questions about whether the "League of Nations," which Wilson proposed at the end of World War I, compromised the United States' sovereignty. But what Wilson had in mind was far from anything like a "one world government." What he wanted was for the United States to assume the responsibility of preserving peace in other lands—in effect, to play "world policeman," protecting all nations from aggression by others.

There was really no hope that without the United States, the most powerful nation in the world, the League could be effective. But after the Senate refused to ratify the Treaty of Versailles that ended the war and set up the League, America turned its back on the world for two decades.

Aggression by Germany, aggression that could have been prevented, was permitted. World War II was the result. America was forced to be the "arsenal of democracy" in another apocalyptic struggle.

From the beaches of Normandy to the sands of Iwo Jima, Americans left their blood on the battlefields of the world and sacrificed their lives on the altar of the rights of man. America stopped Nazi and Fascist totalitarianism.

After World War II, America did not turn its back on the world. From Europe to Asia, the United States restrained a new and more terrible totalitarianism. The United States held the line in Greece and Turkey, in Berlin, in Korea.

America, and America alone, stood in the way of an expanding Communist empire . . .

Until Vietnam.

After the last American helicopter lifted off the roof of our Saigon embassy in 1975, nations one after another, all over the world, fell like dominoes.

23 ★ THE ARK OF THE LIBERTIES OF THE WORLD

And out of his mouth goeth a sharp sword, that with it he should smite the nations, and he shall rule them with a rod of iron; and he treadeth the winepress of the fierceness and wrath of Almighty God.
Revelation 19:15, KJV

Nations, even as individuals, are responsible and accountable to God. The more powerful a nation is, the more responsibility and accountability it has to God.

The United States is one of God's "most favored nations." The other side of the coin is that it is more liable to suffer judgment, as Abraham Lincoln recognized.

In the midst of the Civil War, he issued a proclamation for a day of "national humiliation, fasting, and prayer, recognizing God's hand in the civil strife:

Whereas it is the duty of nations as well as of men to own their dependence upon the overruling power of God, to confess their sins and transgressions in humble sorrow, yet with assured hope that genuine repentance will lead to mercy and pardon, and to recognize the sublime truth, announced in the Holy Scriptures and proven by all history, that those nations only are blessed whose God is the Lord;

And, insomuch as we know that by His divine law nations, like individuals, are subjected to punishments and chastisements in this world, may we not justly fear that the awful calamity of civil war which now desolates the land may be but a punishment inflicted upon us for our presumptuous sins, to the needful end of our national reformation as a people?

Despite the sense of judgment, Lincoln found cause for hope. For the individual, it is never right to do wrong, and so it is for countries. Yet, nations must fight wars. But if they fight for right, they are not so much soldiers as they are policemen for the moral order of the world. If nations do not take responsibility for enforcing the moral law, then who will?

Sometimes it is said that in their foreign policies, nations should not make morality their goal. Statesmen should be "realistic," not "idealistic," and should look only to their own country's self-interest.

But there is really no such neat dichotomy between "realism" and "idealism." The greatest statesmen have understood that in the long if not short run, an amoral foreign policy will not truly serve a nation's interest.

It was no air-headed utopian but Winston Churchill, consummate statesman of the century, who declared the goal of all rational foreign policy: "the permanent prevention of war and the establishment of the conditions of freedom and democracy as rapidly as possible in all countries."

All countries.

When America turns from this mission, it falls into a morass of materialism. America cannot preach one thing at home and practice another thing abroad.

Only if America makes the world safe for democracy, can democracy be safe in America.

America does not need "another Vietnam." May the American people never be asked to fight another war they are forbidden to win.

But America must reassume her responsibilities.

Time is running out. "Over there" is now not so far from our borders.

America is the only power holding back the imperial forces of evil in the world today— America's interests and those of all mankind coincide.

"We Americans are the peculiar, chosen people— the Israel of our time," wrote Herman Melville. "We bear the ark of the liberties of the world." Moreover, "with ourselves, almost for the first time in the history of the earth, national selfishness is unbounded philanthropy; for we cannot do a good to America, but we give alms to the world."[7]

PART FIVE
DECADE OF DESTINY

These are the greatest days of the twentieth century. We have the opportunity to formulate a new beginning for America in this decade. For the first time in my lifetime, we have the opportunity to see spiritual revival and political renewal in the United States. . . . The 1980s are certainly a decade of destiny for America.[1] Jerry Falwell

24 ★ FROM MISSION TO MALAISE

By the mid-seventies, the political activism typical of the sixties had become passé. Apathy was in vogue. *Alienation* became the fashionable word.

War without victory in Vietnam—and the compounded felony of Watergate—pushed national pessimism to epidemic proportions. Across the political spectrum, from left to right, from liberal to conservative, public confidence in government fell dramatically. Polls showed, for example, that nearly two-thirds of the American people trusted government only "some of the time. . . ."

In his Inaugural Address in January 1977, President Jimmy Carter declared, "I have no new dreams to set forth today but rather urge a fresh faith in the old dream." By July 1979, he was proclaiming that "restoring that faith . . . to America is now the most important task we face."

In the summer of 1979, he spent an extraordinary two weeks at Camp David listening "to the voice of America." He had planned yet another speech on the so-called energy crisis. That issue had plagued his presidency nearly from the beginning, and Mr. Carter knew that the nation considered him (as the *Boston Globe* put it) "a disaster as a leader on the energy issue."

Now sensing that his problems went much deeper than energy, he postponed the energy speech and focused on the general condition of his administration and the overall mood of America. Helicopters flew in and out of Camp David daily, delivering new groups of leaders to discuss the state of the nation with President Jimmy Carter. The country waited. It was even rumored that the President had suffered a mental breakdown.

But Congressman Jim Wright of Texas declared, "I prophesy that when the President comes down off the mountain, he will have a comprehensive, effective, hard-hitting program to offer to the American people."

When Jimmy Carter finally came down from the mountain, he revealed his conclusions on television in one of the most unusual presidential speeches of recent history: "All the legislatures in the world can't fix what's wrong with America. I want to talk to you right now about a fundamental threat to American democracy. . . ."

To Carter's understanding, the energy crisis had become a spiritual crisis, "a crisis that strikes at the very heart and soul and spirit of our national will." This crisis could be seen "in the growing doubt about the meaning of our lives and in the loss of unity of purpose for our nation."

The President also sensed that America had lost its momentum as a nation:

> *We always believed that we were part of a great movement of humanity itself called democracy, involved in the search for freedom. And that belief has always strengthened us in our purpose. But just as we are losing our confidence in the future, we are also beginning to close the door on our past.*

He had correctly diagnosed America's deepest problem as "spiritual," though the particular difficulty of that moment in 1979 could have been more accurately described as a "crisis of leadership"—Jimmy Carter's. Ronald Reagan would successfully make that charge in 1980, accusing Carter of blaming the American people for something that was really his own fault.

The great irony of Carter's speech was that the solution he gave for a spiritual problem was a material one—another energy program! "Energy will be the immediate test of our ability to unite this nation," said Carter. "On the battlefield of energy, we can win for our nation a new confidence, and we can seize control again of our common destiny."

A most unlikely scenario, to say the least—solve the spiritual crisis by solving the energy crisis. Many Americans did not even believe that the "energy crisis" was real!

Carter had already correctly identified materialism as a root cause of the American spiritual problem:

In a nation that was proud of hard work, strong families, close-knit communities, and our faith in God, too many of us now tend to worship self-indulgence and consumption. Human identity is no longer defined by what one does, but by what one owns.

But we've discovered that owning things and consuming things does not satisfy our longing for meaning. We have learned that piling up material goods cannot fill the emptiness of lives which have no confidence or purpose.

Such was the problem for which the President proposed an energy-program solution. He also presented another solution: "Let us commit ourselves to a rebirth of the American spirit."

Does the average American really know what "the American spirit" is?

"We simply must have faith," beseeched the President.

But faith in what? Faith in faith?

Carter's solution rang hollow. He seemed to think that faith is like water: when the nation is empty of it, more can be poured back in.

His talk went down in history as the "malaise" speech, though he had not used that actual word. Most Americans probably did not know the difference between "malaise" and mayonnaise!

But they did know that whatever the problem was, neither pious platitudes nor more political programs could quench America's thirst for meaning, revive its sense of destiny, or renew its commitment to a national mission.

25 ★ A MOMENT OF SILENT PRAYER

The "crisis of the American spirit" has many contributing factors.

We have already alluded to one—the Vietnam war. Certainly America's first defeat in a war, along with its turning from its responsibilities as a leader of the free world, has contributed to what Carter called our "crisis of confidence." Other recent events—assassination, resignation, inflation, recession, hostages in Iran—have undoubtedly intensified our national "malaise."

But these are merely symptoms of deeper difficulties.

The "American spirit" is primarily a *vision of the future*—a sense of national destiny and mission rooted in the here-and-now. But the notion of a *national* destiny and mission has no meaning apart from the concept of a *divine* destiny and mission based on eternal values.

At its deepest level, the "crisis of the American spirit" is truly *spiritual in both cause and cure.* Jimmy Carter's successor, an actor-turned-politician (who on the third try finally landed his biggest role and is our strongest President to date since Vietnam and Watergate) has seemed to sense that.

In Detroit, Michigan, on July 17, 1980, before a cast of thousands assembled for the climax of the Republican National Convention, Ronald Reagan departed from his script:

I have thought of something that's not a part of my speech and worried over whether I should do it. Can we doubt that . . . a Divine Providence placed this land, this island of freedom, here as a refuge for all those people in the world who yearn to breathe free? Jews and Christians enduring persecution behind the Iron Curtain; the boat people of Southeast Asia, Cuba and of Haiti; the victims of drought and famine in Africa, the freedom fighters in Afghanistan, and our own countrymen held in savage captivity.

I'll confess that I've been a little afraid to suggest what I'm going to suggest. I'm more afraid not to. Can we begin our crusade joined together in a moment of silent prayer?

God bless America.

There followed high national drama. During that moment of silent prayer, you could have heard a pin drop in the huge hall packed with people. Reagan had just tapped the potential of a *spiritual* appeal to the American people.

26 ★ A SECULAR SOCIETY

In the last half of the twentieth century, America has seemed increasingly to become a "secular society." The Supreme Court, through its controversial decisions on separation of church and state, has contributed significantly to the process of secularization.

The First Amendment, which declares that "Congress shall make no law respecting an establishment of religion, or prohibiting the free exercise thereof," was added to the Constitution in 1791 as part of the Bill of Rights. It was not until 1947 that the Supreme Court proclaimed that the First Amendment "erected a wall of separation between church and state" that "must be kept high and impregnable."[2]

Still later, in 1962, the Court ruled that:

> *... The constitutional prohibition against laws respecting an establishment of religion must at least mean that in this country it is no part of the business of government to compose official prayers for any group of the American people to recite as a part of a religious program carried on by government.*[3]

Then, in 1963, the Court decided that Bible reading as a part of "religious exercises required by the States" violates "the command of the First Amendment that the government maintain strict neutrality, neither aiding nor opposing religion."[4]

To the average American, it seemed that the Supreme Court had outlawed prayer and Bible reading as such in the public schools. In a strictly technical sense, perhaps, that was not what the Justices had done. But to the popular mind, they had erected a "wall of separation," not only between "church and state," but between "God and government" as well.

While great numbers of Americans still profess belief in God—95 percent, according to Gallup polls, the court's church-state decisions have, nevertheless, strongly affected our way of thinking.

Many of us tend to section off religion, drawing a distinction between the "sacred and the secular"—separating religion from our "daily" life as individuals and as a nation, as if there were no connection between God and country and between God and history.

For previous generations, it was the most natural thing in the world to see and speak of "the hand of God in American history." Now that concept has, at best, become a cliché, something we might say when we want to feel or appear to be pious.

Even a candidate for President of the United States may be a little afraid to allude to it, worrying over whether he should even speak of it.

27 ★ THE PRESIDENT AS HIGH PRIEST AND PROPHET

In our government, the president plays many roles: head of state, chief executive, commander-in-chief.

In addition to these strictly constitutional roles, the president in the twentieth century has also come to play the roles of chief legislative leader, head of his party, national crisis manager, and leader of the free world.

But there is yet another presidential role that scholars have neglected.

Teddy Roosevelt called the presidency a "bully pulpit," a platform for speaking out forcefully and for forming public opinion on important issues. That phrase is suggestive of something more.

The president has become what might be called the high priest and prophet of the American civil religion. This may well be the most important presidential role of all.

In playing it, the president strengthens the nation's sense of mission and destiny. Without this national spirit, America can't really be America, and the country falls from mission to malaise.

The first president to play this role to the hilt was Abraham Lincoln. Much has been written of his "political religion," but that term implies that he used religion for political purposes. His utterances were permeated by the language of the King James translation of the Bible. Yet the religion he talked about should more aptly be called, using the terminology developed earlier, the American *civil religion*—a religion neither distinctively Protestant nor Christian, but rather a religion concerning the nation and its future.

At Gettysburg, Lincoln was serving as a kind of priest and prophet of the American civil religion when, with his fellow countrymen, he resolved "that this nation, under God, shall have a new birth of freedom—and that government of the people, by the people, for the people, shall not perish from the earth."

While Lincoln, and later Woodrow Wilson, played this priestly-political role most noticeably and memorably, nearly all the presidents have acted similarly to some extent. Theological concepts, for example, are found in virtually every inaugural address by virtually every president.

In his First Inaugural Address, Washington offered "fervent supplication to that Almighty Being who rules over the universe, who presides in the councils of nations, and whose providential aids can supply every human defect. . . ." He continued by saying, "In tending this homage to the

Great Author of every public and private good, I assure myself that it expresses your sentiments not less than my own, nor those of my fellow-citizens at large less than either." This same Washington could, without being contradictory, later write a Muslim country of North Africa that there was no reason why it and the United States could not enjoy good relations, because America was not per se a "Christian nation"—even though he certainly considered America a nation under God.

A presidential inaugural address of recent memory with remarkable theological emphasis was that of John F. Kennedy, delivered on January 20, 1961. In it he said:

We observe today not a victory of party but a celebration of freedom—signifying renewal as well as change. For I have sworn before you and Almighty God the same solemn oath our forebears prescribed nearly a century and three quarters ago.

The world is very different now. For man holds in his mortal hands the power to abolish all forms of human poverty and all forms of human life. And yet the same revolutionary beliefs for which our forebears fought are still at issue around the globe—the belief that the rights of man come not from the generosity of the state but from the hand of God.

28 ★ SECULAR HUMANISM

The late 1960s gave rise to a new religion in America. Its purpose is to supplant the traditional civil religion of America, along with the accompanying traditional moral consensus. In the name of separation of church and state, this new religion strives to dominate American public life.

This new religion goes by various names—"secularism," "humanism," "secular humanism." Its central tenet is the same: the denial of the existence of God—at least the God in whom so many Americans have believed has assigned a mission and designed a destiny for America.

In his controversial commencement address at Harvard, Alexander Solzhenitsyn termed the new religion "rationalistic humanism or humanistic autonomy: the proclaimed and practiced autonomy of man from any higher force above him . . . with man as the center of all."

Strengthened by the Supreme Court's decisions that have seemed to erect a wall of separation not only between church and state but between God and government as well, "secular humanism" threatens to become a deep mind-set.

So far, "secular humanism" is largely a movement of leftist intellectuals and elitists in the media, education, and government. A broad consensus on traditional values and agreement about America as a nation under God—what we might call a "lower-cased moral majority"—has a long history. It is as old as the country itself, and as recent as the generation to whom President Kennedy spoke. That consensus probably still exists, at least at the grass-roots level.

President Reagan, in his controversial speech of March 8, 1982, in Orlando, Florida, addressed the Forty-first Annual Convention of the National Association of Evangelicals. He warned of "a prevailing attitude of many who have turned to a modern-day secularism, discarding the tried and time-tested values upon which our very civilization is based." He contended that:

No matter how well intentioned, their value system is radically different from that of most Americans. And while they proclaim that they are freeing us from superstitions of the past, they have taken upon themselves the job of superintending us by government rule and regulation. Sometimes their voices are louder than ours, but they are not yet a majority.

29 ★ REAGAN'S RELIGIOUS RHETORIC

President Reagan has been at his best during such moments as the speech at Orlando when, playing the role of high priest and prophet of the American civil religion, he has bucked the secular trends of our day and kicked up a storm of controversy. Since the beginning of his political career, critics have insisted he is unqualified for high public office because of his background as a Hollywood movie actor. In point of fact, his acting experience and flair for drama, his sense of what moves men's souls, may be the very factors that have made him uniquely qualified for the presidency—especially in a time when a revival of national spirit and traditional religious and moral convictions is needed.

Reagan's religious rhetoric may be a key element in what has to be called the first successful presidency since Watergate and Vietnam. When playing the role of high priest and prophet, a president must reach deep down to the religious roots of our American soul, and lift us up to follow his leadership. Reagan has brought to politics what he terms "a commitment to freedom and personal liberty that, itself, is grounded in the much deeper realization that freedom prospers only where the blessings of God are avidly sought and humbly accepted."

In Orlando, President Reagan declared:

The American experiment in democracy rests on this insight. Its discovery was the great triumph of our Founding Fathers, voiced by William Penn when he said: "If we will not be governed by God, we must be governed by tyrants." Explaining the inalienable rights of men, Jefferson said, "The God who gave us life gave us liberty at the same time." And it was George Washington who said that "of all the dispositions and habits which lead to political prosperity, religion and morality are indispensable supports."

And finally, that shrewdest of all observers of American democracy, Alexis de Tocqueville, put it eloquently after he had gone on a search for the secret of America's greatness and genius: "Not until I went into the churches of America and heard her pulpits aflame with righteousness did I understand the greatness and the genius of America. America is good. And if America ever ceases to be good, America will cease to be great."

30 ★ THE EVIL EMPIRE

At Orlando, the President renewed his commitment to many of the causes upon which he had based his 1980 campaign. Here he pledged again to work against abortion on demand (the consequence of the 1973 *Roe v. Wade* Supreme Court decision). He also promised to seek a constitutional amendment restoring prayer to public schools.

Anticipating the inevitable "But you're violating the First Amendment and separation of church and state" charge, Reagan declared that "freedom prospers when religion is vibrant and the rule of law under God is acknowledged."

"When our Founding Fathers passed the First Amendment, they sought to protect churches from government interference," he argued.

They never intended to construct a wall of hostility between government and the concept of religious belief itself. The evidence of this permeates our history and our government. The Declaration of Independence mentions the Supreme Being no less than four times. "In God We Trust" is engraved on our coinage. The Supreme Court opens its proceedings with a religious invocation. And the members of Congress open their sessions with a prayer. I just happen to believe the school children of the United States are entitled to the same privileges as Supreme Court justices and congressmen.

The President was in an upbeat mood in Orlando. "There is a great spiritual awakening in America," he proclaimed, "a renewal of the traditional values that have been the bedrock of America's goodness and greatness."

To prove his point, he cited a recent survey that showed Americans "far more religious than the people of other nations," with "95 percent of those surveyed" expressing "a belief in God and a huge majority" believing "the Ten Commandments had real meaning in their lives." He noted another study that found "an overwhelming majority of Americans" disapproving "of adultery, teen-age sex, pornography, abortion and hard drugs," and showing "a deep reverence for the importance of family ties and religious belief."

As the President approached the end of his speech, his tone became more somber and dramatic: "There is sin and evil in the world. And we are enjoined by Scripture and the Lord Jesus to oppose it with all our might."

"Our nation, too," continued the President, "has a legacy of evil with which it must deal." Ronald Reagan realizes that America is not perfect—it never has been nor will it ever be.

The glory of America, however, lies in "its capacity for transcending the moral evils of our past," the President pointed out. He gave as an example "the long struggle of minority citizens for equal rights, once a source of disunity and civil war," but "now a point of pride for all Americans." Then, in a declaration that reminds us of Woodrow Wilson's warning that "we cannot turn back," he declared, "We must never go back."

Nearing the climax of his speech, when he turned to foreign affairs and national security, his rhetoric became increasingly Wilsonian and visionary.

Whatever sad episodes exist in our past, any objective observer must hold a positive view of American history, a history that has been a history of hope fulfilled and dreams made into reality. Especially in this century, America has kept alight the torch of freedom, not just for ourselves, but for millions of others around the world.

The President told his Christian audience to "pray for the salvation of all of those who live in that totalitarian darkness—pray that they will discover the joy of knowing God." But until that happens, he warned, let all beware that those who "preach the supremacy of the state, declare its omnipotence over individual man, and predict its eventual domination of all peoples of the Earth—they are the focus of evil in the modern world."

Christians must see the evil in communism, Reagan urged, and view the struggle between West and East as a "struggle between right and wrong and good and evil," recognizing that "Marxism-

Leninism is actually the second oldest faith proclaimed in the Garden of Eden with the words of temptation, 'Ye shall be as gods.' "

"Yes, change your world," he challenged, then quoted Tom Paine: "We have it within our power to begin the world over again." In the trumpet-blasting, drum-rolling, cymbal-clashing finale, the President reminded his hearers of "the fact of history and the aggressive impulses of an *evil empire*...."

At the end, there was anything but silence. The band played "Onward Christian Soldiers," and the audience leaped to its feet.

Predictably, there was also anything but silence in the press regarding what has come to be known as Reagan's "Darth Vader" speech ("Darth Vader" is the leader of the "evil empire" in *Star Wars*).

President Reagan had dared to call evil *evil*. He had dared to suggest that even though church and state are and must be separate, God and government must always be together.

But there was new cause for hope for those Americans who believe that if the nation is to meet the challenge of advancing Soviet communism, then the great spirit of national mission must be revived. Communism believes that "history" is on its side and that its victory is inevitable. Only an America that believes in its divine destiny can withstand such a foe.

31 ★ EAST OF EDEN

"Modern man is, it seems, faced by the final challenge of history," concludes Ernest Lee Tuveson in *Redeemer Nation: The Idea of America's Millennial Role*. That is to "create the millennium, or go down into the lake of fire."[5]

Of course, creating the "millennium" exceeds our human power alone. After the Fall, perfection became out of reach for man forever. We live permanently east of Eden.

There will be war until the Prince of Peace comes again, and some slavery and tyranny until he reigns. Perhaps "Pug" was right when, at the end of the television version of Herman Wouk's *The Winds of War*, he pondered that in this strife-torn century, only the Second Coming of Christ can set things right.

Yet, lowered expectations of the future must be no excuse for letting evildoers get away with doing as much evil in the world as they will.

Whether the flag of freedom will be flying anywhere on the earth when the year 2000 dawns depends on what America does now.

What would the world be like if "the focus of evil in the modern world" were allowed unlimited conquest or continued aggression to the point that, backed into a corner, we choose to be "dead rather than Red"? In either case, the world would be hell on earth.

But imagine the world freed from the threat of domination by the "evil empire" Soviet Russia and other nations with similar goals.

America and other nations could beat their swords into plowshares . . .

All the treasure and genius now harnessed for war could be marshaled for good . . .

No countries would face external obstacles to democracy and human rights . . .

Liberty and democracy would reign from pole to pole. . . .

After all that, the question remains: Is it America's destiny to deliver the world from tyranny?

32 ★ A NEW DAWNING FOR AMERICA

Halfway through the 1980s we are in what Jerry Falwell has called "a decade of destiny for America."[6] It is already clear that ours is a decade of debate over whether America even has a destiny, and if so, what it is.

The "decline of America" has become a common topic for political leaders, media pundits, and even futuristic novelists. In Paul Erdman's best-selling novel *The Last Days of America,* for example, the hero explains to a group of Europeans what has gone wrong with America:

For the first time in our history, we have totally lost our momentum as a nation. And momentum was the key, I believe, to the success of the United States. It always had to be heading somewhere, its people had to believe that that somewhere was good and part of our nation's manifest destiny, and they had to further believe that God would grant them leadership which would lead them into that promised land safe and sound....[7]

Set in 1985, *The Last Days of America* is fiction, but very perceptive fiction, and all too true in its analysis of America's current predicament.

Deep down, most Americans would probably like to believe that God has a purpose for America, but America is stuck in the mire of despair. It needs "to back up so it can go forward."

The present generation needs to understand that its questions are nothing new. They have been asked before. And history gives hope that answers are attainable.

The battle for Planet Earth in the final decades of the twentieth century will not be decided by military might alone. It is a war of ideas, too.

Our adversaries know what they believe and why they believe it. They are atheists, but are driven by a kind of religious fervor.

Though we may match their military might, missile for missile, what will we gain if we win the world but lose our soul as a nation? Nothing.

It took the Great Awakening to lay the groundwork for the American Revolution. And it will take another spiritual revival to recreate another "revolution in religion" and renew our "religion of revolution."

Is it possible? Who would be so bold as to limit God and say that it is *not* possible? "These are the greatest days of the twentieth century. We have the opportunity to formulate a new beginning for America in this decade," declares Reverend Jerry Falwell. "For the first time in my lifetime, we have the opportunity to see spiritual and political renewal in the United States."[8]

There is yet time for America to claim the promise of its revolutionary destiny.

To fight for a planetary civilization of free peoples and independent democratic nations, with human rights for all . . .

To be the liberator of mankind and the leader of revolutionary progress in the world . . .

To be the launching pad for the evangelization of the world before the Second Coming of Christ . . .

The twentieth century has been called "the American century," but God may not be finished with America yet.

When the year 2000 dawns, the story of the greatest nation in the history of the world may have just begun.

NOTES

INTRODUCTION
1. George Bancroft, *History of the United States*, 10 vols. (Boston: Little, Brown, and Co., 1856), I: 4.

PART ONE
1. Charles F. Adams, *The Works of John Adams* (Boston: Little, Brown, and Co., 1856), X: 282-83.
2. Jonathan Edwards, *Faithful Narrative of the Surprising Work of God, The Works of Jonathan Edwards* (Edinburgh: Banner of Truth Trust, 1974), I: 348.
3. *Ibid.*, p. 348.
4. Alexis de Tocqueville, *Democracy in America*, ed. Phillips Bradley (New York: Alfred A. Knopf, 1963), I: 308.
5. Jonathan Edwards, *A History of the Work of Redemption, The Works of Jonathan Edwards* (Edinburgh: Banner of Truth Trust, 1974), I: 617.
6. *Ibid.*, p. 616.
7. Adams, *The Works of Adams*, pp. 282-283.
8. Calvin Coolidge, "Religion and the Republic," *Foundations of the Republic* (New York: Books for Libraries Press, 1968), p. 150.

9. Francis Bradley, *The American Proposition; A New Type of Man* (New York: Moral Re-armament, 1977), p. 37, and Lee Vrooman, *The Faith That Built America* (New York: Arrowhead Books, 1955), p. 69.

PART TWO

1. Kate L. Roberts, comp., *Hoyt's New Cyclopedia of Practical Quotations* (New York: Funk and Wagnalls Co., 1922), p. 825.
2. *Ibid.*, p. 825.
3. Gresham Machen, "Christianity and Liberty," *The Forum* (March 1931), pp. 162-64.
4. John Locke, *Second Treatise of Civil Government*, ed. Thomas P. Peardon (Indianapolis: Bobbs-Merrill Co., 1952), p. 5.
5. John Locke, *The Reasonableness of Christianity*, ed. I. T. Ramsey (Stanford, Cal.: Stanford University Press, 1958), pp. 60-61.
6. Locke, *Second Treatise*, pp. 5-6.
7. Cline Hall and Jerry Combee, "The Moral Majority: Is It a New Ecumenicalism?" *Foundations*, XXV (No. 2), 207, especially note 23.

PART THREE

1. Alexis de Tocqueville, *Democracy in America*, eds. J. P. Mayer and Max Lerner (New York: Harper and Row, 1966), p. 24.
2. Alexis de Tocqueville, *Democracy in America*, ed. Phillips Bradley (New York: Alfred A. Knopf, 1963), I: 6-7.
3. *Ibid.*, p. 14.
4. *Ibid.*, p. 308.
5. *Ibid.*, p. 308.
6. *Ibid.*, pp. 303-304.
7. See Footnote 4, Part I.
8. *Ibid.*, pp. 305-306.
9. Noah Webster, *History of the United States* (New Haven: Durrie and Peck, 1832), pp. 273-74.
10. Kenneth Scott Latourette, *History of Christianity* (New York: Harper and Company, 1953), p. 1063.
11. B. H. Carroll, *An Interpretation of the English Bible: Revelation* (Grand Rapids: Baker Book House, 1973), p. 219.
12. *Ibid.*, pp. 219-220.
13. *Eerdmans' Handbook to the History of Christianity* (Grand Rapids, Mich.: Wm. B. Eerdmans Publishing Co., 1977), p. 519.
14. Russel Blaine Nye, *Society and Culture in America, 1830–1860* (New York: Harper Torchbooks, 1974), p. 36.
15. *Ibid.*, p. 296.

NOTES

16. *Ibid.*, p. 37.
17. *Ibid.*, p. 36.
18. *Ibid.*, p. 287.
19. Charles B. Finney, *Revivals of Religion* (Virginia Beach: CBN University Press, 1978), pp. 311-12.
20. *Ibid.*, p. 312.
21. Robert Handy, *A Christian America: Protestant Hopes and Historical Realities* (New York: Oxford University Press, 1971), p. 48.
22. *Ibid.*, p. 49.
23. *Ibid.*, p. 50.
24. *Ibid.*, p. 66.
25. *Ibid.*, p. 66.
26. *Ibid.*, p. 66.

PART FOUR
1. Henry Steele Commager, ed., *Documents of American History*, 8th ed. (New York: Appleton-Century-Crofts, 1968), II: 132.
2. Ernest Lee Tuveson, *Redeemer Nation: The Idea of America's Millennial Role* (Chicago: University of Chicago Press, 1968), p. 78.
3. *Ibid.*, p. 25.
4. Russel Blaine Nye, *Society and Culture in America, 1830–1860* (New York: Harper Torchbooks, 1974), p. 17.
5. Tuveson, *Redeemer Nation*, p. 133.
6. Robert Handy, *A Christian America: Protestant Hopes and Historical Realities* (New York: Oxford University Press, 1971), p. 185.
7. Tuveson, *Redeemer Nation*, pp. 156-57.

PART FIVE
1. Jerry Falwell, "Future-Word: An Agenda for the Eighties," in *The Fundamentalist Phenomenon*, ed. Jerry Falwell (Garden City, New York: Doubleday and Co., Inc., 1981), p. 186.
2. *Everson v. Board of Education*, 330 U.S. 1(1947).
3. *Engle v. Vitale*, 370 U.S. 421(1962).
4. *Abingdon Township School District v. Schempp*, 374 U.S. 203(1963).
5. Ernest Lee Tuveson, *Redeemer Nation: The Idea of America's Millennial Role* (Chicago: University of Chicago Press, 1968), p. 231.
6. Falwell, *Fundamentalist Phenomenon*, p. 186.
7. Paul Erdman, *The Last Days of America* (New York: Pocket Books, 1981), p. 167.
8. Falwell, *Fundamentalist Phenomenon*, p. 186.

APPENDIX
Speech by President Ronald Reagan
Forty-First Annual Convention of the
National Association of Evangelicals
Sheraton Twin Towers Hotel, Orlando, Florida
March 8, 1983

Those of you in the National Association of Evangelicals are known for your spiritual and humanitarian work. And I would be especially remiss if I didn't discharge right now one personal debt of gratitude.

Thank you for your prayers. Nancy and I have felt their presence many times in many ways. And believe me, for us they've made all the difference.

The other day in the East Room of the White House at a meeting there, someone asked me whether I was aware of all the people out there who were praying for the President and I had to say, "Yes, I am. I've felt it. I believe in intercessory prayer." But I couldn't help but to say to that questioner after he'd asked the question—or at least say to them—that if sometimes when he was praying he got a busy signal, it was just me in there ahead of him.

I think I understand how Abraham Lincoln felt when he

said, "I have been driven many times to my knees by the overwhelming conviction that I had nowhere else to go."

From the joy and the good feeling of this conference, I go to a political reception. Now, I don't know why, but that bit of scheduling reminds me of a story which I'll share with you.

An evangelical minister and a politician arrived at Heaven's gate one day together. And St. Peter, after doing all the necessary formalities, took them in hand to show them where their quarters would be. And he took them to a small single room with a bed, a chair, and a table and said this was for the clergyman.

The politician was a little worried about what might be in store for him. And he couldn't believe it when St. Peter stopped in front of a beautiful mansion with lovely grounds and many servants and told him that these would be his quarters. And he couldn't help but ask, "But wait—there's something wrong—how could I get this mansion while that good and holy man only gets a single room?"

And St. Peter said, "You have to understand how things are up here. We've got thousands and thousands of clergy. You're the first politician who ever made it."

But I don't want to contribute to a stereotype.

So I tell you there are a great many God-fearing, dedicated, noble men and women in public life, present company included. And, you, we need your help to keep us ever mindful of the ideas and the principles that brought us into the public arena in the first place. The basis of those ideas and principles is a commitment to freedom and personal liberty that, itself, is grounded in the much deeper realization that freedom prospers only where the blessings of God are avidly sought and humbly accepted.

The American experiment in democracy rests on this insight. Its discovery was the great triumph of our Founding Fathers, voiced by William Penn when he said: "If we will not be governed by God, we must be governed by tyrants." Explaining the rights of men, Jefferson said, "The God who gave us life gave us liberty at the same time." And it was George Washington who said that "of all the dispositions and habits which lead to political prosperity, religion and morality are indispensable supports."

And finally, that shrewdest of all observers of American democracy, Alexis de Tocqueville, put it eloquently after he had gone on a search for the secret of America's greatness and genius:

Not until I went into the churches of America and heard her pulpits aflame with righteousness did I understand the greatness and the genius of America. America is good. And if America ever ceases to be good, America will cease to be great.

Well, I am pleased to be here today with you who are keeping America great by keeping her good. Only through your work and prayers and those of millions of others can we hope to survive this perilous century and keep alive this experiment in liberty, this last, best hope of man.

I want you to know that this Administration is motivated by a political philosophy that sees the greatness of America in you her people, and in your families, churches, neighborhoods, communities—the institutions that foster and nourish values like concern for others and respect for the rule of law under God.

Now, I don't have to tell you that this puts us in opposition to, or at least out of step with, a prevailing attitude of many who have turned to a modern-day secularism, discarding the tried and time-tested values upon which our very civilization is based. No matter how well intentioned, their value system is radically different from that of most Americans. And while they proclaim that they are freeing us from superstitions of the past, they have taken upon themselves the job of superintending us by government rule and regulation. Sometimes their voices are louder than ours, but they are not yet a majority.

An example of that vocal superiority is evident in a controversy now going on in Washington. And since I'm involved, I've been waiting to hear from the parents of young America. How far are they willing to go in giving to government their prerogatives as parents?

Let me state the case as briefly and simply as I can. An organization of citizens sincerely motivated and deeply concerned about the increase in illegitimate births and abortions involving girls well below the age of consent sometime ago established a nationwide network of clinics to offer help to these girls and hopefully alleviate this situation.

Now again, let me say, I do not fault their intent. However, in their well-intentioned effort, these clinics have decided to provide advice and birth control drugs and devices to underage girls without the knowledge of their parents.

For some years now, the federal government has helped with funds to subsidize these clinics. In providing for this, the Congress declared that every effort would be made to maximize parental participation. Nevertheless, the drugs and devices are prescribed without getting parental consent or giving notification after they've done so. Girls termed "sexually active"—and that has replaced the word "promiscuous"—are given this help in order to prevent illegitimate birth or abortion.

We have ordered clinics receiving federal funds to notify the parents when such help has been given. One of the nation's leading newspapers has created the term "squeal rule" in editorializing against us for doing this, and we're being criticized for violating the privacy of young people. A judge has recently granted an injunction against an enforcement of our rule.

I've watched TV panel shows discuss this issue, seen columnists pontificating on our error, but no one seems to mention morality as playing a part in the subject of sex.

Is all of Judeo-Christian tradition wrong? Are we to believe that something so sacred can be looked upon as a purely physical thing with no potential for emotional and psychological harm? And isn't it the parents' right to give counsel and advice to keep their children from making mistakes that may affect their entire lives?

Many of us in government would like to know what parents think about this intrusion in their family by government. We're going to fight in the courts. The rights of parents and the rights of family take precedence over those of Washington-based bureaucrats and social engineers.

But the fight against parental notification is really only one example of many attempts to water down traditional values and even abrogate the original terms of American democracy. Freedom prospers when religion is vibrant and the rule of law under God is acknowledged. When our Founding Fathers passed the First Amendment, they sought to protect churches from government interference. They never intended to construct a wall of hostility between government and the concept of religious belief itself.

The evidence of this permeates our history and our government. The Declaration of Independence mentions the Supreme Being no less than four times. "In God We Trust" is engraved on our coinage. The Supreme Court opens its proceedings with a religious invocation. And the members of Congress open their sessions with a prayer. I just happen to believe the school children of the United States are entitled to the same privileges as Supreme Court justices and congressmen.

Last year, I sent the Congress a constitutional amendment to restore prayer to public schools. Already this session, there's growing bipartisan support for the amendment, and I am calling on the Congress to act speedily to pass it and to let our children pray.

Perhaps some of you read recently about the Lubbock school case where a judge actually ruled that it was unconstitutional for a school district to give equal treatment to religious and non-religious student groups, even when the group meetings were being held during the students' own time. The First Amendment never intended to require government to discriminate against religious speech.

Senators Jeremiah Denton and Mark Hatfield have proposed legislation in the Congress on the whole question of prohibiting discrimination against religious forms of student speech. Such legislation could go far to restore freedom of religious speech for public school students. And I hope the Congress considers these bills quickly. And with your help, I think it's possible we could also get the constitutional amendment through the Congress this year.

More than a decade ago, a Supreme Court decision literally wiped off the books of fifty states statutes protecting the rights of unborn children. Abortion-on-demand now takes the lives of up to one-and-one-half million unborn children a year. Human life legislation ending this tragedy will someday pass the Congress, and you and I must never rest until it does. Unless and until it can be proven that the unborn child is not a living entity, then its right to life, liberty, and the pursuit of happiness must be protected.

You may remember that when abortion-on-demand began, many of you warned that the practice would lead to a decline in respect for human life, that the philosophical premises used to justify abortion-on-demand would ultimately be used to justify other attacks on the sacredness of human life, infanticide or mercy killings. Tragically enough, those warnings proved all too true: only last year a court permitted the death by starvation of a handicapped infant.

I have directed the Health and Human Service Department to make clear to every health care facility in the United States that the Rehabilitation Act of 1973 protects all handicapped persons against discrimination based on handicaps, including infants. And we have taken the further step of requiring that each and every recipient of federal funds who provides health care services to infants must post and keep posted in a conspicuous place a notice stating that "discriminatory failure to feed and care for handicapped infants in this facility is prohibited by federal law." It also lists a twenty-four hour, toll-free number so that nurses and others may report violations in time to save the infant's life.

In addition, recent legislation introduced in the Congress by Representative Henry Hyde of Illinois not only increases restrictions on publicly financed abortion or infanticide. It urges the Congress to begin hearings and to adopt legislation that will protect the right of life to all children, including the disabled or handicapped.

Now, I'm sure that you must get discouraged at times, but you've done better than you know, perhaps. There is a great spiritual awakening in America—a renewal of the traditional values that have been the bedrock of America's goodness and greatness. One recent survey by a Washington-based research council concluded that Americans were far more religious than the people of other nations; 95 percent of those surveyed expressed a belief in God and a huge majority believed the Ten Commandments had real meaning in their lives.

And another study has found that an overwhelming

majority of Americans disapprove of adultery, teenage sex, pornography, abortion, and hard drugs. And this same study showed a deep reverence for the importance of family ties and religious belief.

I think the items that we've discussed here today must be a key part of the nation's political agenda. For the first time the Congress is openly and seriously debating and dealing with the prayer and abortion issues—and that's enormous progress right there. I repeat: America is in the midst of a spiritual awakening and a moral renewal, and with your biblical keynote I say today, "Yes, let justice roll on like a river, righteousness like a never failing stream."

Now, obviously, much of this new policy and social consensus that I have talked about is based on a positive view of American history, one that takes pride in our country's accomplishments and record. But we must never forget that no government schemes are going to perfect man. We know that living in this world means dealing with what philosophers would call the phenomenology of evil or, as theologians would put it, the doctrine of sin.

There is sin and evil in the world. And we are enjoined by Scripture and the Lord Jesus to oppose it with all our might. Our nation, too, has a legacy of evil with which it must deal. The glory of this land has been its capacity for transcending the moral evils of our past.

For example, the long struggle of minority citizens for equal rights, once a source of disunity and civil war, is now a point of pride for all Americans. We must never go back. There is no room for racism, anti-semitism, or other forms of ethnic and racial hatred in this country.

I know that you have been horrified, as have I, by the resurgence of some hate groups preaching bigotry and prejudice. Use the mighty voice of your pulpits and the powerful standing of your churches to denounce and isolate these hate groups in our midst. The commandment given us is clear and simple: "Thou shalt love thy neighbor as thyself."

But whatever sad episodes exist in our past, any objective observer must hold a positive view of American history, a history that has been the story of hopes fulfilled and dreams made into reality. Especially in this century, America has kept alight the torch of freedom, not just for ourselves, but for millions of others around the world.

And this brings me to my final point today. During my first press conference as President, in answer to a direct question, I pointed out that, as good Marxist-Leninists, the Soviet leaders have openly and publicly declared that the only morality they recognized is that which will further their cause, which is world revolution.

I think I should point out, I was only quoting Lenin, their guiding spirit who said in 1920 that they repudiate all morality that proceeds from supernatural ideas—that is their name for religion—or ideas that are outside class conceptions Morality is entirely subordinate to the interests of class war. And everything is moral that is necessary for the annihilation of the old exploiting social order and for uniting the proletariat.

Well, I think the refusal of many influential people to accept this elementary fact of Soviet doctrine illustrates an historical reluctance to see totalitarian powers for what they are. We saw this phenomenon in the 1930s. We see it too often today. This does not mean we should isolate ourselves and refuse to seek an understanding with them.

I intend to do everything I can to persuade them of our peaceful intent, to remind them that it was the West that refused to use its nuclear monopoly in the forties and fifties for territorial gain and which now proposes 50 percent cuts in [its] entire class of land-based intermediate-range nuclear missiles.

At the same time, however, they must be made to understand we will never compromise our principles and standards. We will never give away our freedom. We will never abandon our belief in God. And we will never stop searching for a genuine peace, but we can assure none of these things America stands for, through the so-called nuclear freeze solutions proposed by some.

The truth is that a freeze now would be very dangerous fraud, for that is merely the illusion of peace. The reality is that we must find peace through strength.

I would agree to a freeze if only we could freeze the Soviet's global desires. A freeze at current levels of weapons would remove any incentive for the Soviets to negotiate seriously in Geneva, and virtually end our chances to achieve the major arms reductions which we have proposed. Instead, they would achieve their objective through the freeze.

A freeze would reward the Soviet Union for its enormous and unparalleled military buildup. It would prevent the essential and long overdue modernization of United States and allied defenses and would leave our aging forces increasingly vulnerable. And an honest freeze would require extensive prior negotiations on the systems and numbers and compliance. And the kind of a freeze that has been suggested would be virtually impossible to verify. Such a major effort would divert us completely from our current negotiations on achieving substantial reductions.

A number of years ago, I heard a young father, a very prominent young man in the entertainment world, addressing a tremendous gathering in California. It was during the time of the Cold War, and communism and our own way of life were very much on people's minds. And he was speaking to that subject. And suddenly I heard him saying, "I love my little girls more than anything. . . ." And I said to myself, "Oh, no, don't. You can't say that." But I had underestimated him. He went on: "I would rather see my little girls die now, still believing in God, than have them grow up under communism and one day die no longer believing in God."

There were thousands of young people in that audience. They came to their feet with shouts of joy. They had instantly recognized the profound truth in what he had said, with regard to the physical and the soul and what was truly important.

Yes, let us pray for the salvation of all of those who live in that totalitarian darkness—pray that they will discover the joy of knowing God. But until they do, let us be aware that while they preach the supremacy of the state, declare its omnipotence over individual man, and predict its eventual domination of all peoples on the Earth—*they* are the focus of evil in the modern world.

It was C. S. Lewis who, in his unforgettable *Screwtape Letters*, wrote:

The greatest evil is not done now in those sordid "dens of crime" that Dickens loved to paint. It is not even done in concentration camps and labor camps. In those we see its final result. But it is conceived and ordered (moved, seconded, carried, and minuted) in clear, carpeted, warmed, and well-lighted offices, by quiet men with white collars and cut fingernails and smooth-shaven cheeks who do not need to raise their voices.

Because these "quiet men" do not "raise their voices," because they sometimes speak in soothing tones of brotherhood and peace, because, like other dictators before them, they're always making "their final territorial demand," some would have us accept them at their word and accommodate ourselves to their aggressive impulses. But, if history teaches anything, it teaches that simple-minded appeasement or wishful thinking about our adversaries is folly. It means the betrayal of our past, the squandering of our freedom.

So I urge you to speak out against those who would place the United States in a position of military and moral inferiority. You know, I've always believed that old Screwtape reserved his best efforts for those of you in the church. So, in your discussions of the nuclear freeze proposals, I urge you to beware the temptation of pride—the temptation of blithely declaring yourselves above it all and labeling both sides equally at fault, to ignore the facts of history and the aggressive impulses of an evil empire, to simply call the arms race a giant misunderstanding and thereby remove yourself from the struggle between right and wrong and good and evil.

I ask you to resist the attempts of those who would have you withhold your support for our efforts, this Administration's efforts, to keep America strong and free, while we negotiate real and verifiable reductions in the world's nuclear arsenals and one day, with God's help, their total elimination.

While America's military strength is important, let me add here that I have always maintained that the struggle now going on for the world will never be decided by bombs or rockets, by armies or military might. The real crisis we face today is a spiritual one; at root, it is a test of moral will and faith.

Whittaker Chambers, the man whose own religious conversion made him a witness to one of the terrible traumas of our time, the Hiss-Chambers case, wrote that the crisis of the Western world exists to the degree in which the West is indifferent to God. And then he said, "For Marxism-Leninism is actually the second oldest faith first proclaimed in the Garden of Eden with the words of temptation, 'Ye shall be as gods.' "

"The Western world can answer this challenge," he wrote, "but only provided that its faith in God and the freedom He enjoys is as great as communism's faith in man."

I believe we shall rise to the challenge. I believe that communism is another sad, bizarre chapter in human history whose last pages even now are being written. I believe this because the source of our strength in the quest for human freedom is not material but spiritual. And because it knows no limitation, it must terrify. And ultimately in the words of Isaiah: "He giveth power to the faint; and to them that have no might he increased strength. . . . But they that wait upon the Lord shall renew their strength; they shall mount up with wings as eagles; and shall run and not be weary. . . ."

Yes, change your world. One of our Founding Fathers, Thomas Paine, said, "We have it within our power to begin the world over again." We can do together what no one church could do by itself. God bless you and thank you very much.